PRAISE F...

PIRATE ENLIGHTENMENT,
OR THE REAL LIBERTALIA

)

"*Pirate Enlightenment* pluralizes and globalizes our understanding of whose ideas and actions are considered impactful and whose vision shapes the world, a framing that still resonates in contemporary times . . . In his academic writing and political commitments, David Graeber exemplified an ethos of action and conversation . . . As anthropologists have noted, gifts are inalienable—they contain within them something of the giver. Graeber's final book is certainly such a gift."   —Jatin Dua, *Science*

"A tour de force of anthropological scholarship and an important addition to Malagasy history . . . Certain to be controversial, but all the more important for that."   —*Kirkus Reviews*

"A characteristically radical rereading of history that places the social and political experiments of pirates at the heart of the European Enlightenment. A brilliant companion volume to the bestselling *Dawn of Everything*."

—Amitav Ghosh, author of *Smoke and Ashes*

"Daring, carefully speculative, and intellectually ambitious: all qualities that we have come to expect of the late David Graeber. *Pirate Enlightenment* is a splendid example of Graeber's transformative and convincing case that the Enlightenment was a cosmopolitan and plebian concoction, fabricated far from the European centers of Enlightenment thought."

—James C. Scott, Sterling Professor of Political Science and professor of anthropology at Yale University

"Radical, magical, and enchanting: a true history of a people's Enlightenment, led by Malagasy women and egalitarian pirates at a crossroads of the world—a land of battle, foment, and booty, whose inhabitants liked nothing better than pranking outsiders to spread outlandish tales of their lives."

—Cory Doctorow, author of *Walkaway* and coauthor of *Chokepoint Capitalism*

"In *The Dawn of Everything*, David Graeber urged historically minded scholars to consider the ways that human beings have continually pursued three basic freedoms, including the freedom to create new forms of social relations. In this book, he provides a fascinating example of the transformative potential of this proposition. Showing how rumored eighteenth-century 'pirate kingdoms' established in Madagascar can be understood from the perspective of the local Malagasy population, Graeber gives us a glimpse of people—men and women—taking control of the society in which they live, making new forms of sociality. *Pirate Enlightenment* is, as the author writes, a provocation—but also an inspiration—and a great piece of storytelling."

—Rosemary A. Joyce, interim director of Global, International, and Area Studies and distinguished professor of anthropology at the University of California, Berkeley

Marijan Murat

DAVID GRAEBER

PIRATE ENLIGHTENMENT, OR THE REAL LIBERTALIA

David Graeber was a professor of anthropology at the London School of Economics. He is the author of *Debt: The First 5,000 Years* and *Bullshit Jobs: A Theory*, among many other books, and the coauthor, with David Wengrow, of the *New York Times* bestseller *The Dawn of Everything*. He was an iconic thinker and a renowned activist, and his early efforts in Zuccotti Park made Occupy Wall Street an era-defining movement. He died in 2020.

ALSO BY DAVID GRAEBER

The Dawn of Everything:
A New History of Humanity (with David Wengrow)

Bullshit Jobs: A Theory

On Kings (with Marshall Sahlins)

The Utopia of Rules:
On Technology, Stupidity, and the Secret Joys of Bureaucracy

The Democracy Project: A History, a Crisis, a Movement

Debt: The First 5,000 Years

Direct Action: An Ethnography

Lost People: Magic and the Legacy of Slavery in Madagascar

Fragments of an Anarchist Anthropology

Toward an Anthropological Theory of Value:
The False Coin of Our Own Dreams

PIRATE

ENLIGHTENMENT,

OR THE REAL LIBERTALIA

DAVID GRAEBER

PICADOR

FARRAR, STRAUS AND GIROUX

NEW YORK

Picador
120 Broadway, New York 10271

Originally published in French in 2019 by Libertalia Press, France,
as *Les pirates des lumières*
Published in the United States in 2023 by Farrar, Straus and Giroux
First paperback edition, 2024

Library of Congress Control Number: 2022043530
Paperback ISBN: 978-1-250-32187-9

Designed by Patrice Sheridan

Our books may be purchased in bulk for promotional, educational, or business
use. Please contact your local bookseller or the Macmillan Corporate and
Premium Sales Department at 1-800-221-7945, extension 5442, or by
email at MacmillanSpecialMarkets@macmillan.com.

Picador® is a U.S. registered trademark and is used by Macmillan Publishing Group,
LLC, under license from Pan Books Limited.

For book club information, please email marketing@picadorusa.com.

picadorusa.com • Follow us on social media at @picador or @picadorusa

1 3 5 7 9 10 8 6 4 2

CONTENTS

PREFACE

THIS ESSAY WAS FIRST WRITTEN TO BE A CHAPTER OF A COL-
lection of essays about divine kingship that I coauthored with
Marshall Sahlins. When I had been carrying out my original
field research in Madagascar between 1989 and 1991, I first
learned not only that many of the Caribbean pirates had settled in Madagascar, but, even more, that their descendants
remained there as a self-identified group (a fact I discovered
when I was briefly romantically involved with a woman whose
ancestry harked back to Sainte-Marie). Later I was startled by
the fact that no one had ever carried out systematic field research among them. I even made plans, at one point in my
life, to carry out a fieldwork project among them—plans that
ended up short-circuited by life contingencies of one sort or
another and never came to fruition. Someday I still might
do it. I acquired a photocopy around that time of the Mayeur manuscript, after a visit to the British Library, which for
a very long time sat in a pile of books and documents near a

large picture window in the room in which I'd grown up in my apartment in New York, on extremely large sheets of paper, barely legible in its eighteenth-century handwriting. For many years I often felt it was slightly reproachfully beckoning to me from across the room as I was trying to work on something else. Then when I lost my home to the machinations of Police Intelligence in 2014, I had the whole thing scanned, along with various family pictures and documents too bulky to bring with me to London, and eventually, I arranged to have it transcribed.

It was always something of a mystery to me that the text itself had never been published: especially since the British Library original, which had been composed in Mauritius, contained a little note explaining that a typescript version of the text could be found in the Académie Malgache in Antananarivo, and that if one wished to view it, one should consult with a certain M. Valette. Several essays by French authors who had clearly consulted with, and summarized, portions of this typescript had appeared, but the original manuscript—a scholarly tome in its own right, replete with numerous critical footnotes—never had.

Eventually I realized I had accumulated enough material on the pirates to make an interesting essay in itself. The original title—since it was supposed to be in an essay for a book on kings—was "Pirate Enlightenment: The Mock Kings of Madagascar," the subtitle being a reference to a short book by Daniel Defoe about Henry Avery. In the process of writing, however, the essay grew and grew. Before long it was a good seventy single-spaced pages, and I began to seriously wonder both whether it would make the resulting compendium itself too long and whether the subject matter had drifted too far away from the original emphasis on fraudulent kings (and larger questions of whether all kings were in a sense impostors, with the differences between them being only matters of degree) to really justify inclusion.

In the end I decided: everyone hates a long essay; everyone loves a short book. Why not turn the essay into a freestanding work and let it stand on its own merits?

And that is what I have done.

)

The opportunity to publish the book with Libertalia Press proved impossible to resist. The image of Libertalia, the utopian pirate experiment, has remained an endless source of inspiration for those on the libertarian left; it has always been felt that even if it did not exist, it should have existed; or even if it did not exist in any literal sense, even if there was never any actual settlement that bore that name, the very existence of pirates and pirate societies was itself a kind of experiment, and that even at the deepest origins of what has come to be known as the Enlightenment project, one now seen in revolutionary quarters as a false dream of liberation that has instead unleashed unspeakable cruelty upon the world, there was a kind of redemptive promise of a genuine alternative.

Intellectually, this small book can be seen as one contribution to a larger intellectual project that I first laid out in an essay called "There Never Was a West" (which also

appeared as a small freestanding book in French), and that
I'm now pursuing as part of a joint project with the British
archaeologist David Wengrow. In the language currently fash-
ionable, it might be referred to as a project of "decolonizing
the Enlightenment." There can be no doubt that many of the
ideas we now see as products of the eighteenth-century European Lumières were, indeed, used to justify extraordinary
cruelty, exploitation, and destruction, not just on the working
classes at home, but on those who lived on other continents.
But the blanket condemnation of Enlightenment thought is
in its own way rather odd, when one considers that this was
perhaps the first historically known intellectual movement organized largely by women, outside of official institutions like
universities, with the express aim of undermining all existing
structures of authority. What's more, if one examines many of
the original sources, Enlightenment thinkers were often quite
explicit that the sources of their ideas lay outside what we now
call "the Western tradition" entirely. To take one example,
which will be developed in another book, in the 1690s, just
around the time the pirates were establishing themselves in
Madagascar, there was something of a proto-Enlightenment
salon being held in Montreal in the home of the Comte
de Frontenac, then governor of Canada, in which he and his
assistant, Lahontan, debated questions of social importance—
Christianity, economics, sexual mores, etc.—with a Huron
statesman named Kandiaronk, who took the position of an
egalitarian and skeptical rationalist and held that the punitive
apparatus of European law and religion was made necessary
only by an economic system arranged in such a way that it would

inevitably produce precisely the behaviors that apparatus was designed to repress. Lahontan was later to release his own redaction of his notes from some of these debates as a book, in 1704, and that book rapidly became a bestseller across Europe. Almost every major Enlightenment figure ended up writing an imitation of it. Yet somehow, figures like Kandiaronk have been written out of history. No one denies these debates actually happened; rather, the assumption is always that when it came time to write up accounts of what happened, men like Lahontan simply ignored everything Kandiaronk actually said and substituted some kind of "noble savage fantasy" drawn entirely from the European intellectual tradition. In other words, we have projected backward the idea that there was a self-contained "Western civilization" (a concept that didn't even really exist until the early twentieth century) and, with a genuinely perverse irony, used accusations of racial arrogance on the part of those we designate "Westerners" (basically now a euphemistic code word for "white people") as a pretext to exclude everyone not designated "white" from having any influence on history, and intellectual history in particular. It's as if history, and especially radical history, has become some sort of moral game where all that's really important is to make clear just how much one is not letting the Great Men of history off the hook for the (obviously, very real) racism, sexism, and chauvinism they displayed, without somehow noticing that a four-hundred-page book attacking Rousseau is still a four-hundred-page book about Rousseau.

I still recall as a child being very impressed by an interview with the Sufi writer Idries Shah, who remarked how curious

it was that so many intelligent and decent human beings in
Europe and America spent so much of their time in protest
marches chanting the names and waving pictures of people
that they hated ("Hey hey, LBJ, how many kids did you kill
today?"). Didn't they realize, he remarked, how incredibly grat-
ifying that was to the politicians they were denouncing? It was
remarks like that, I think, that eventually caused me to reject
a politics of protest and embrace one of direct action.

Some of the indignation that can be traced in this essay
flows from this. Why do we not see a man like Kandiaronk as
an important theorist of human freedom? He clearly was. Why
do we not see a man like Tom Tsimilaho as one of the pioneers
of democracy? Why have the contributions of the women who
we know played such important roles in Huron and Betsimisaraka society, but whose very names have largely been lost,
been excluded even from the stories we do tell about such
men—as, for that matter, the women who organized the
salons have largely been excluded from the story of the Enlightenment itself?

If nothing else, what I'd like this little experiment in historical writing to bring home is that existing history is not just
deeply flawed and Eurocentric, it's also unnecessarily tedious
and boring. There is a surreptitious pleasure in moralism, yes,
just as there is a kind of mathematical glee to be found in
reducing all human action to self-aggrandizing calculation.
But these are ultimately tawdry pleasures. The real story of
what happened in human history is a thousand times more
diverting.

Let us tell, then, a story about magic, lies, sea battles,

purloined princesses, slave revolts, manhunts, make-believe kingdoms and fraudulent ambassadors, spies, jewel thieves, poisoners, devil worship, and sexual obsession that lies at the origins of modern freedom. I hope the reader has as much fun as I did.

)

The first Greeks were all pirates.
—Montesquieu, *The Spirit of the Laws*

This is a book about pirate kingdoms, real and imagined. It's also about a time and place where it is very difficult to tell the difference between the two. For about a hundred years, from the end of the seventeenth century toward the close of the next, the east coast of Madagascar was scene to a shadow play of storied pirate kings, pirate atrocities, and pirate utopias, rumors of which shocked, inspired, and entertained the clients of cafés and pubs across the North Atlantic world. There is absolutely no way, from our current vantage, to disentangle these accounts and establish a definitive narrative of which were true and which were not.

Some clearly weren't. In the first decade of the eighteenth century, for instance, many in Europe believed that a great kingdom had been created in Madagascar by a certain Captain Henry Avery and ten thousand pirate henchmen, a kingdom that was on the verge of establishing itself as one of the world's preeminent naval powers. In fact, this kingdom did not exist. It was a hoax. Most historians are now convinced

the same could be said of the story of the great utopian experiment of Libertalia, a story also set in Madagascar, which
appears in a chapter of a certain Captain Johnson's *A General
History of the Pyrates* in 1724. Johnson describes Libertalia as
an egalitarian republic, in which slavery had been abolished
and all things were shared in common and administered dem-
ocratically, created by a retired French pirate captain named
Misson under the philosophical influence of a defrocked Ital-
ian priest. But historians have found no other evidence that
either a pirate captain named Misson or such a defrocked
priest (his name is given as Caraccioli) actually existed—
despite the fact that almost all the other pirates mentioned
in the book *can* be documented from archival sources. Similarly, archaeologists have been unable to locate any evidence
for the physical existence of Libertalia. As a result, the general
consensus is that the whole story is simply made up. Some
are willing to allow it might have been a sailor's legend that
the author of *History of the Pyrates* just felt was too good not
to include, even though he presumably knew the events in
question never really happened. Most simply Captain Johnson
(whoever he was) fabricated the entire incident. Few, however,
seem to feel it matters much, one way or the other, because
the only important question is assumed to be: "Was there ever
really a utopian settlement of former pirates called Libertalia
on the Malagasy coast?"

To my mind, this is a rather trivial question. It would appear likely there was no Misson or Caraccioli, or a settlement
with precisely that name; but there most certainly were pirate
settlements on the Malagasy coast, and what's more, they were

the place for radical social experiments. Pirates did experiment with new forms of governance and property arrangements; what's more, so did members of the surrounding Malagasy communities into which they married, many of whom had lived in their settlements, sailed in their ships, formed blood brotherhood pacts, and spent many hours in political conversation with them. One way the story of Captain Misson is indeed deceptive is that it arranges the story in such a way that the Malagasy are kept out of it, providing the pirates with shipwrecked foreign wives and reducing the surrounding people to hostile tribes who eventually overwhelm and kill them. But this just makes it easier for historians and anthropologists to do what they are inclined to do anyway in such circumstances: that is, to treat the political affairs of those identified as Europeans, and those identified as African or anyway nonwhite, as entirely separate domains of inquiry, separate worlds, which were unlikely to have any serious political, let alone intellectual, influence, one on the other.

In fact, as we'll see, the reality was much more complicated. But also much more interesting and hopeful.

So: stories about Libertalia, or for that matter Avery's pirate kingdom, were in no sense isolated fantasies. What's more, their very existence and popularity was a historical phenomenon in its own right. In a certain sense these stories might even be said, to adopt Marx's phrase, to be a material force in history. After all, the Golden Age of Piracy, as it's now called, really lasted only forty or fifty years; it was quite some time ago; but people all over the world are still telling stories about pirates and pirate utopias—or for that matter, elaborating on them with the kinds of kaleidoscopic fantasies about magic, sex, and death that, as we'll see, have always accompanied them. It's hard to escape the conclusion that these stories endure because they embody a certain vision of human freedom, one that still feels relevant—but one, at the same time, that offers an alternative to the visions of freedom that were to be adopted in European salons over the course of the eighteenth century, and that still remain dominant today. The toothless or peg-legged buccaneer hoisting a flag of defiance against the world, drinking and feasting to a stupor on stolen loot, fleeing at the first sign of serious opposition, leaving only tall tales and confusion in his wake, is, perhaps, just as much a figure of the Enlightenment as Voltaire or Adam Smith, but he also represents a profoundly proletarian vision of liberation, necessarily violent and ephemeral. Modern factory discipline was born on ships and on plantations. It was only later that budding industrialists adopted those techniques of turning humans into machines into cities like Manchester and Birmingham. One might call pirate legends, then, the most important form of poetic expression produced by that emerging North Atlantic proletariat whose exploitation laid the ground for the industrial revolution.* As long as those forms of discipline, or their more subtle and insidious modern incarna-

---

* It was Eric Williams (*Capitalism and Slavery*) who first developed the idea that European slave plantations in the New World were, in effect, the first factories; the idea of a "pre-racial" North Atlantic proletariat, in which these same techniques of mechanization, surveillance, and discipline were applied to workers on ships, was elaborated by Peter Linebaugh and Marcus Rediker (*The Many-Headed Hydra*).

tions, govern our working lives, we will always fantasize about buccaneers.

This is not, however, primarily a book about the romantic appeal of piracy. It is a work of history, informed by anthropology; an attempt to establish what actually happened on the northeast coast of Madagascar at the end of the seventeenth century and the beginning of the eighteenth when several thousand pirates made that place their home, and to make a case that in a broader sense Libertalia did exist, and that it could indeed be considered, in a sense, the first Enlightenment political experiment. And that many of the men and women who brought this experiment into being spoke Malagasy.

)

There is no doubt that stories about pirate utopias circulated widely, and that they did have historical effects. The real question is just how widely, and how profound, those effects actually were. I think a good case can be made that they were extremely important. For one thing, these stories began circulating very early, in the time of Newton and Leibniz, long before, say, the emergence of the political theory that came to be identified with Montesquieu and the Encyclopedists. Montesquieu of course made the argument that all nations first emerged as something very like utopian experiments: great lawgivers imposed their visions, laws came to constitute the character of great nations. In stories such men had undoubtedly heard in their childhood and adolescence, pirate captains like Misson or Avery had been represented as attempting to do exactly that. In 1707, when Montesquieu was precisely eighteen years old, Daniel Defoe was writing a broadside in England that compared the pirates settling Madagascar to the founders of ancient Rome, brigands who established themselves in a new territory, created new laws, and eventually grew to become a great conquering nation. That much of this excitement surrounding such pronouncements was due to wildly inflated propaganda or even outright fraud doesn't make much difference in terms of how such matters were received. We don't know if that particular screed was translated into French (it probably wasn't), but we do know that men claiming to represent the new pirate kingdom did visit Paris around the same time, seeking some kind of alliance. Did the young Montesquieu hear about this? Again, we don't know, but it's hard to imagine it wasn't just the sort of news that students at the time were joking and arguing about, and that was most likely to catch the imagination of an ambitious young intellectual.

Some things we do know. Perhaps it might be good to start by listing them. We know that a very large number of seventeenth-century pirates, from the Caribbean and elsewhere, settled along the northeast coast of Madagascar, where their Malagasy descendants ("the Zana-Malata") remain a self-identified group to this day. We know that their arrival set off a series of social upheavals that ultimately led to the formation, in the early eighteenth century, of a political entity called the Betsimisaraka Confederation. We also know that those who live in the territory once controlled by this confederation—a coastal strip almost seven hundred kilometers long—still refer to themselves as Betsimisaraka and are considered one of

Madagascar's most stubbornly egalitarian peoples. We know the man who is considered to be the founder of this confederation was named Ratsimilaho, that Ratsimilaho was said at the time to be the son of an English pirate from a settlement called Ambonavola (most likely the town now known as Foulpointe), and that Ambonavola is described in contemporary English accounts as itself a kind of utopian experiment, an attempt to apply the democratic principles of organization typical of pirate ships to a settled community on land. Finally, we know that Ratsimilaho was eventually declared King of the Betsimisaraka in that very city.

All of this we can say with a fair degree of certainty. Beyond this, though, our sources become extremely confusing. The accepted chronology, for instance, established in the colonial period, holds that Ratsimilaho reigned as King of the Betsimisaraka from 1720 to 1756. Accounts written two generations later represent him as a kind of Enlightenment philosopher king who created the Betsimisaraka from his own personal genius, but whose ambitious plans to introduce European science and civilization were ultimately frustrated by the eventual defeat of his pirate allies and depredations of French slave traders. This, however, is extremely difficult to square with accounts written at the time, which represent this same person—or what at any rate appears to be the same person—sometimes as a king, but also sometimes as just one of a collection of local chiefs, and in one case as the second-in-command for a Jamaican pirate "king" named John Plantain. Another account represents him as the second-in-command for a Malagasy monarch in an entirely different part of the country.

What's more, archaeologists have found no evidence that there actually was a Betsimisaraka kingdom, in any recognizable sense of the term, at all; states that were created in other parts of Madagascar at the time show distinct material traces, but along the northeast coast there is no evidence of the building of palaces and public works, creation of systems of taxation, hierarchies of officials, or standing armies, or of any significant disruption to older patterns of rural life.

What is one to make of all this?

In this small book I might not be able to provide a comprehensive explanation of the existing evidence—that might well be impossible anyway—but I will attempt to provide a general framework within which it might be interpreted. There are several points at which my analysis breaks with conventional understandings of the period.

First of all, I'll argue that in Madagascar at the time, and particularly in areas influenced by the pirates, stories of mighty kingdoms, or even the actual existence of what looked like royal courts, should not necessarily be taken at face value. All the materials existed on the coast at the time to set up Potemkin courts to impress outsiders, and it's quite clear that at least some of the "kings" encountered by foreign observers were simply playing a game of make-believe, with the active complicity of their ostensible Malagasy retainers. Pirates were particularly good at such games. In fact, one reason the Golden Age of Piracy remains the stuff of legend is that pirates of that age were so skilled at manipulating legends; they deployed wonder-stories—whether of terrifying violence or inspiring ideals—as something very much like weapons of war, even if the war in question was the desperate and ultimately doomed struggle of a motley band of outlaws against the entire emerging structure of world authority at the time.

Second of all, I would emphasize that like all successful propaganda, these stories did contain elements of truth. The republic of Libertalia may not have existed, at least in any literal sense, but pirate ships, pirate towns like Ambonavola, and, I would argue, the Betsimisaraka Confederation itself— which was created by Malagasy political actors working in close tandem with the pirates—were in many ways self-conscious experiments in radical democracy. I would even go so far as to suggest that they did indeed represent some of the first stirrings of Enlightenment political thought, exploring ideas and principles that were ultimately to be developed by political philosophers and put in practice by revolutionary regimes a century later. This anyway would explain the apparent paradox of the Betsimisaraka: supposedly created by a failed philosopher king but, in fact, remaining as a stubbornly egalitarian people to this day, notorious, in fact, for their refusal to accept the authority of overlords of any sort.

THE (VERY) RADICAL ENLIGHTENMENT

Calling this volume "pirate Enlightenment" is obviously something of a provocation. All the more so since nowadays the Enlightenment itself has fallen into disrepute. While the Lumières of the eighteenth century thought of themselves as radicals, engaged in an attempt to break with all shackles of received authority to lay the foundations of a universal theory of human freedom, contemporary radical thinkers are more likely to see Enlightenment thought as the ultimate in received authority, as an intellectual movement whose main achievement was to lay the foundations of a peculiarly modern form of rational individualism that became the basis of "scientific" racism, modern imperialism, exploitation, and genocide. There is no doubt that this is indeed what happened when European imperialists, colonialists, and slave owners raised on Enlightenment ideas were let loose upon the world. Of course one might also argue about causality here. Would such men have behaved any differently had they still been justifying their behavior (as they had in centuries previous) in terms of religious faith? Most likely not. But it seems to me (and I have suggested this elsewhere)[1] that much of the ensuing debate distracts us from a much more fundamental question: whether Enlightenment ideals, and particularly Enlightenment ideals of human liberation, can be meaningfully called "Western" at all. Because I strongly suspect that when future historians look back at such matters, they are likely to conclude that most were not. The European Enlightenment was, more than anything else, an age of intellectual synthesis where previously intellectual backwaters like England and France that suddenly found themselves at the center of global empires, and exposed to (for them) startling new ideas, were trying to integrate, for instance, ideals of individualism and liberty drawn from the Americas, a new conception of the bureaucratic nation-state largely inspired by China, African contract theories, and economic and social theories originally developed in medieval Islam.

Insofar as there was a practical synthesis going on—that is, insofar as anyone, especially in the early days of the Enlightenment, was experimenting with new ways of organizing social relations in light of all these new ideas—it was for obvious reasons, happening not in the great cities of Europe, still under the control of various ancien régimes, but on the margins of the emerging world-system, and particularly in the relatively free spaces that often opened up alongside imperial adventures, with all the rearrangement of peoples alongside them that they so often entailed. These were often side effects of terrible violence, the destruction of existing peoples and civilizations. But it's important to remember this isn't all they were. I have already made note, if somewhat in passing,[2] of the importance of pirates in all this, particularly in spearheading the development of new forms of democratic governance, showing that pirate crews were so often made up of so many different sorts of people with knowledge of so many different kinds of social arrangements (the same ship might include Englishmen, Swedes, escaped African slaves, Caribbean Creoles, Native Americans, and Arabs), committed to a certain rough-and-ready egalitarianism, tossed together in situations where the rapid creation of new institutional structures was absolutely required, that they were in a sense perfect laboratories of democratic experiment. At least one prominent historian of European political thought has indeed suggested that some of the democratic forms later developed by Enlightenment statesmen in the North Atlantic world most likely were first debuted on pirate ships in the 1680s and 1690s:

> That leadership could derive from the consent of the led, rather than be bestowed by higher authority, would have been a likely experience of the crews of pirate vessels in the early modern Atlantic world. Pirate crews not only elected their captains, but were familiar with countervailing power (in the forms of the quartermaster and ship's council) and contractual relations of individual and collectivity (in the form of written ship's articles specifying shares of booty and rates of compensation for on-the-job injury).[3]

It was no doubt the novelty of such forms that inspired British and French authors to begin fantasizing about pirate utopias like Libertalia to begin with. But in those accounts, the principal actors are always Europeans. The story of Libertalia is a case in point. We only know of it from a book called *A General History of the Pyrates*, which appeared in 1724 under the name of Captain Charles Johnson, which was probably a pseudonym of Daniel Defoe. The settlers, all of European stock, set about creating a kind of liberal experiment, based on majority vote and private property, but also the abolition of slavery, racial divisions, and organized religion; almost every truly famous pirate (Tom Tew, Henry Avery, etc.), was said to have joined in the effort; the story ends when they are attacked and overwhelmed by restless natives, who destroy them for no discernible reason. So despite the pretense of racial equality, the Malagasy do not take part. Natives, in such accounts, are never the sort of people who would engage in political experiments themselves. And in fact, this (ultimately racist) bias continues in the colonial, and even most contemporary, historiography. Political experiments carried out by those speaking European languages are treated as entirely unrelated to political experiments carried out by those speaking the Malagasy language, even if they were conducted in almost exactly the same time and place and by actors in daily contact with one another.

Insofar as received historical wisdom allows the pirates any influence on the creation of the Betsimisaraka Confederation, for example, it is assumed to be literally genetic. The Betsimisaraka, the standard history goes, was created by the children of European pirates and Malagasy mothers, under the inspired leadership of a single particularly charismatic Malata named Ratsimilaho, imposed over the passive Malagasy natives, who simply beckoned to his call. What's more, Ratsimilaho is always represented as essentially importing already-existing European inventions, such as the nation-state, and never making any political contribution of his own. The French historian Hubert Deschamps states the conventional wisdom of the colonial period, which remains more or less the conventional wisdom to this day:

> Such was the great man, that child of a pirate, who imposed himself as prince by his intelligence and character. He was able to group together the scattered tribes of the East Coast, who had lived in anarchy, war, and misery.

He made of them a powerful and prosperous state, assuring its persistence and cohesion . . .

He was the first to introduce to the Grand Island the
territorial sense of a state, of which the European countries no doubt offered him an example . . . [But] after
him, his kingdom decomposed bit by bit.[4]

In fact, almost none of this standard view stands up to
scrutiny. First of all, as we will see, while Ratsimilaho clearly
did exist, and does appear to have been the son of a local
Malagasy woman named Rahena and an English pirate named
Thamo or Tom, the rest of the Malata were mostly children
at the time that the confederation was created.* Further, the
sources we have make it quite clear that other than Ratsimilaho himself, those who were adults refused to have anything
to do with it.

Second of all, there is no evidence Ratsimilaho's kingdom was anything even remotely like a "territorial state." In
fact, there's no real evidence for the existence of a kingdom
of any sort. An archaeological survey of the region[5] reports
no change in settlement patterns after the creation of the
"kingdom"—and certainly, neither archaeologists nor anyone
else has detected evidence of anything like an administrative
hierarchy or system of social classes in the northeast at the
time. All evidence suggests most decisions continued to be

---

* Not only that, none could have been over roughly twenty-one when the war
began in 1712, since no significant number of pirates were operating in Madagascar until roughly 1691. Ratsimilaho himself is said to have been eighteen
at the time.

made, as they always had been, in popular assemblies in which all concerned with the outcome had a right to speak their piece. In fact, as we'll see, there is good reason to believe that political and social organization was actually *less* hierarchical, after the creation of the "kingdom," than it was before: since the ranked grades of warrior aristocrats alluded to in earlier accounts disappear. Hence the assemblies became if anything more important. True, the Zana-Malata did gradually become something more or less like an intermarrying hereditary aristocracy, who went back to their ancestors' pirate ways and organized raids on the Comoro Islands—and even Zanzibar— at century's end; but they were always considered fundamentally external to society, and their political power was ultimately broken by a popular uprising around the same time the territory was being incorporated into the highlands-based kingdom of Madagascar in 1817.[6]

We would seem to be in the presence of a genuine historical anomaly: a political entity that presented itself to the outside world as a kingdom, organized around the charismatic figure of a brilliant child of pirates, but which within operated by a decentralized grassroots democracy without any developed system of social rank. How to explain this? Are there any real historical analogies?

In fact, the most obvious parallel would be pirate ships themselves. Pirate captains often tried to develop a reputation among outsiders as terrifying, authoritarian desperadoes, but on board their own ships not only were they elected by majority vote and could be removed by the same means at any time, they were also empowered to give commands only during chase or combat, and otherwise had to take part in the assembly like anybody else. There were no ranks on pirate ships, other than the captain and the quartermaster (the latter presided over the assembly). What's more, we know of explicit attempts to translate this form of organization onto the Malagasy mainland. Finally, as we'll see, there is a long history of buccaneers or other questionable characters who found themselves a foothold in some Malagasy port town, trying to pass themselves off as kings and princes without doing anything to reorganize actual social relations on the ground in the surrounding communities.*

The Betsimisaraka, then, did reorganize actual social relations in their communities. They simply did not do so in the way one would under an actual monarchy.

What I'm going to argue in this book is that the advent of the pirates might be said to have set off a series of revolutions on the coast. The first and probably the most important of these revolutions was spearheaded largely by women, and it was aimed at breaking the ritual and economic power of the clan that had previously been the intermediaries between foreigners and the peoples of the northeast coast. The creation of the Betsimisaraka Confederation was in fact the second, and might best be viewed as a kind of male backlash against the

---

* The original subtitle of the essay on which this book was based, for example, was inspired by a little book by Daniel Defoe, *The King of Pirates: Being an Account of the Famous Enterprises of Captain Avery, the Mock King of Madagascar* (1720). For a brief period, Avery, or his agents, or perhaps people just pretending to be his agents, managed to convince even some of the crowned heads of Europe that he was the founder of an ambitious new pirate kingdom on the island.

first. Under the cover of the pirates, and the formal leadership of a half-caste pirate king, clan leaders and ambitious young warriors carried out what I think would best be considered their own proto-Enlightenment political experiment, a creative synthesis of pirate governance and some of the more egalitarian elements in traditional Malagasy political culture. What is generally written off as a failed attempt to create a kingdom can just as easily be seen as a successful Malagasy-led experiment in pirate Enlightenment.

PART I

PIRATES AND MOCK KINGS OF THE MALAGASY NORTHEAST

It is very hard to be objective about pirates. Most historians don't even try. The literature on seventeenth-century piracy is largely divided between romantic celebrations, in the popular literature, and scholarly debates over whether pirates would be best viewed as protorevolutionaries, or as simple murderers, rapists, and thieves.[1] I don't really want to wade into all this here. Anyway, there were all sorts of pirates. Some of the men remembered as pirate captains were actually gentleman freebooters, privateers, official or unofficial agents of one or another European regime; others might well have been mere nihilistic criminals; but many did indeed create, however briefly, a kind of rebel culture and civilization that, though surely brutal in many ways, developed its own moral code and democratic institutions. Perhaps the best that could be said of them is that their brutality was in no way unusual by the standards of their time, but their democratic practices were almost completely unprecedented.

It's also this latter group—the sorts of pirates most appreciated by radical historians—who appear to be of most immediate relevance to what happened in seventeenth- and eighteenth-century Madagascar.

A little background is in order then.

Some early pirate ships were privateers gone rogue, but typically, pirate crews were born in mutiny. Discipline on board sixteenth-century European ships was arbitrary and brutal, so crews often had good reason to rise up; but the law on land was unforgiving. A mutinous crew knew they had signed their own death warrants. To go pirate was to embrace this fate. A mutinous crew would declare war "against the entire world," and hoist the "Jolly Roger." The pirate flag, which existed in many variations, is revealing in itself. It was normally taken to be an image of the devil, but often it contained not only a skull or skeleton, but also an hourglass, signifying not a threat ("you are going to die") so much as a sheer statement of defiance ("we are going to die, it's only a matter of time")—which crews making out such a flag on the horizon would likely have found, if anything, even more terrifying. Flying the Jolly Roger was a crew's way of announcing they accepted they were on their way to hell.

It might be worth pausing for a moment to consider how seriously this kind of defiance—not just of law, but of God—was taken in the North Atlantic world of the seventeenth century. To embrace the devil was no casual business. By the nautical standards of the times, theft, violence, and cruelty were par for the course; blasphemy, and the systematic rejection of religion, was another matter. While sailors' speech was, then as now, known to be colorful, among pirates it often seemed to pass into a veritable ideology. Hell constantly beckoned. Certainly this was what outside observers invariably emphasized. Clement Downing's history of a pirate named John Plantain begins:

> John Plantain was born in Chocolate Hole, on the Island of Jamaica, of English Parents, who took care to bestow on him the best Education they themselves were possess'd of: which was to curse, swear, and blaspheme, from the time of his first learning to speak.[2]

The same author, himself a sailor, records his horror at witnessing his crew, on an anti-pirate expedition, being greeted by Malagasy villagers with enthusiastic cries of "God damn ye, John! Me love you!"—the villagers having learned their English from the pirates.[3]

Plantain himself was later to establish himself for a time in Madagascar, where he became known as "the King of Ranter Bay." Scholars have long been intrigued by the title. While "Ranter Bay" seems to just be an Anglicization of the Malagasy Rantabe ("big beach"), it also seems hard to imagine it's not a reference to the Ranters, a radical working-class antinomian movement that two generations before had openly preached the abolition of private property and existing sexual morality. (Blasphemy laws had in fact been largely introduced in England to suppress them.) While there's no historical evidence of Ranters' ideas having a direct influence on the buccaneers,*

---

* In an essay called "Radical Pirates?," Christopher Hill (*People and Ideas in Seventeenth-Century England*) suggests antinomians, including Radical Quakers and Ranters, who took refuge in Jamaica or other Caribbean colonies, might have influenced the pirates, or even become pirates, but this remains speculation.

if nothing else this gives a sense of the kind of associations they evoked in the minds of their contemporaries. These were men (the Indian Ocean pirates were almost exclusively male) who lived in a kind of space of death, who were seen by the law-abiding as hell-bound, if not fiends themselves, committed to a perverse embrace of their own demonization.

PIRATES COME TO MADAGASCAR

Buccaneers of what's come to be known as the Golden Age of Piracy began in the Atlantic, preying on shipping from the New World: the last remains of the Spanish treasure fleets, and the new wealth coming from the plantation economies of the West Indies. Gradually, many discovered that the Indian Ocean, with its European and Asian merchant vessels loaded with spices, silks, and precious metals, afforded much richer prey. Especially tempting prizes were to be found in the Red Sea among Muslims from India and beyond on pilgrimage to Mecca. Madagascar was the ideal base for such raids because it existed in a sort of legal gray zone: the island was not included in the purview of the British Royal African Company, which organized the Atlantic slave trade, but it also fell outside the jurisdiction of the East India Company. While powerful kingdoms existed on the west coast, and to some degree in the south, the northeast was wide-open, and afforded numerous natural harbors: what were later to grow into the port towns of Fenerive, Tamatave, Foulpointe, and Sainte-Marie.

Sainte-Marie, or Saint Mary, is actually the name given by

European traders to an island just south of the Bay of Antongil, which had been a common point of call for explorers
and marauders since at least the 1650s. Malagasy refer to it as
Nosy Boraha. The island is notable for having a good supply
of water and a well-protected harbor, which after 1691 became
a notorious pirate base, with fortress, refitting center, and em-
porium, replete with a small town whose population might
fluctuate, depending on the season, between a few score and
well over a thousand active and retired freebooters, runaways,
and escapees of one sort or another, along with their various
Malagasy wives, allies, merchants, and hangers-on.

The founder of the town of Sainte-Marie was a man named
Adam Baldridge, himself a former pirate wanted for murder in
Jamaica, who found himself a position as the commercial agent
of an extremely successful, but notoriously unscrupulous, New
York merchant named Samuel Philipse. Philipse already knew
the area; he had engaged in commissioning ships to purchase
slaves on the island in the late 1680s, and this allowed him to
pretend that he was establishing a post for "legitimate" commerce (slaves), when in fact the post served largely to supply
the buccaneers and dispose of their booty. For a while this
resulted in a vigorous trade between Sainte-Marie and New
York. Ships making the "pirate round" from the Caribbean
to the Indian Ocean would invariably stop at Sainte-Marie,
often to careen their ship and resupply with food and weapons, then, if successful, return to sell off loot. Crew members
wishing to take a break from seafaring, or attempt to return
home incognito, would sojourn off there; some would take up
permanent residence.

Baldridge was master of the fort and sometimes liked to refer to himself as "the Pirate King," but there's no evidence that anyone else did, or that in dealing with other buccaneers he was really much more than first among equals. The town seems to have had no stable government, or even population: this is because for most it was a place of temporary respite; those who did intend to stay longer often ended up dying fairly quickly of tropical disease exacerbated by drunkenness and other indulgences; those who did survive usually ended up settling on the mainland. Over time, the number of retired pirates did increase to several thousand, and the northeast coast was speckled with little pirate settlements.

THE PROBLEM WITH BOOTY

It's impossible to understand the importance of Sainte-Marie unless one bears in mind that, while pirates operating in the Red Sea often found themselves in possession of enormous amounts of cash, along with gold, jewels, silks and calicoes, ivory, opium, and other exotic products, they often found it quite difficult to dispose of the stuff. One could no more, in the 1690s, walk into a London jeweler's shop with a large bag full of diamonds and collect, say, a hundred thousand pounds in cash than one could today; the disposal of sums so large, especially by men from obviously modest backgrounds, would immediately attract the attention of the criminal authorities. The larger the sum, the more of a problem it became. Histories regularly report that after a given haul members of a pirate crew ended up in possession of treasure worth £120,000, and dutifully calculate how many millions this would be worth today, but it was well-nigh impossible for a pirate to translate such sums into, say, a stately seaside mansion on the coast of Cornwall, or Cape Cod. Perhaps one could find a corrupt or venal colonial official in the West Indies or Réunion who might offer the life of a settler for the lion's share of the booty; but otherwise one would have to construct elaborate schemes or false identities just to be able to cash in a portion of the loot.

The case of Henry Avery (aka Henry Every, aka Ben Bridgeman, aka Long Ben), who secured perhaps the greatest haul in pirate history, is instructive. Avery had been elected captain of a privateer called the *Charles* after the crew mutinied in May 1694.[4] Making their way to the Indian Ocean, they ended up joining a squadron that attacked a convoy of heavily armed Mughal ships on the way to Mecca, taking two (the *Ganj-i-Sawai* and *Fateh Muhammed*) after prolonged chase and battle, and making off with an estimated haul of £600,000 (according to the claim the Mughal court was later to make on the English authorities). According to one popular version of the story, Avery was the first of the crew to figure out that the jewels covering the furniture on the ships were not just cut glass, and while his crew were gathering up gold and coins, he went about with a chisel securing himself a sackful of diamonds. This is almost certainly a legend; in fact, the treasures were duly shared out among the crew; but disposing of the loot became an intractable problem. Apparently with objects of such value, Baldridge couldn't help them. As a result, some men departed to Réunion, the ship itself first headed to Nassau, where the governor was rumored to be corruptible.

The problem was that the haul was simply too fantastic. An outraged Aurangzeb, accusing the British government of complicity, seized East India representatives in the country and threatened to expel them; the British government duly declared Avery an "enemy of all mankind" and an international manhunt was announced—the world's first. Some of Avery's men scattered across the North American colonies; others returned under assumed names to Ireland; a few were discovered trying to unload their goods, some of those ratted out their companions; and in the end, twenty-four were arrested and six publicly hanged in an attempt to appease the Mughal government. Avery's fate, however, remained a mystery. He was never apprehended. Some said he died in hiding a short time later. Others insisted that he did eventually find himself a way to cash in, and retired in comfort, perhaps somewhere in the tropics; yet others, that he was systematically fleeced by Bristol diamond merchants, who knew a wanted man couldn't take them to court no matter what they did, and died many years later, a pauper in some seaside slum, unable to afford even a coffin for his funeral.

Still, it would be too simplistic to conclude that Avery's international notoriety was simply a burden. The legends that soon surrounded him afforded any number of later pirates, and perhaps Avery himself (we really don't know what happened to him), the means to figure out a more advantageous way to negotiate with the existing power structure: by claiming to be representatives of a pirate kingdom. Rumors soon began to flow, in many cases clearly encouraged by Sainte-Marie pirates themselves, that Avery was still in Madagascar—that, in fact, he had made off with the Mughal's daughter, who had fallen in love with the dashing buccaneer after the *Ganj-i-Sawai* was taken, and that they had founded a new kingdom in Madagascar. Some described Avery as ruling the island from an impregnable fortress with his princess bride, or presiding over a utopian democratic experiment in which all goods were shared in common. (These were the stories that morphed into Libertalia.) Before long, envoys of this imaginary pirate state appeared at courts across Europe, describing a burgeoning new kingdom dominating the southwest Indian Ocean, with thousands of pirates and confederates of all nations, with a vast fleet of warships, seeking allies. They approached the British court in 1707, and the French and Dutch courts in 1712 and 1714, respectively. In these cases they saw little success, but then a few years later won a much more receptive ear in Russia, the Ottoman Empire, and Sweden. The Swedish government actually signed initial treaties and prepared to send an ambassador before discovering the ruse; Peter the Great contemplated using alliance with the pirates to establish a Russian colony on Madagascar.[5]

Of course, we can have no way to know if these "envoys" were in any way connected with actual pirates, or were just independent scam artists. But the stories made a profound impact on the European imagination. One of the first writers to take up the cause of the new pirate state was a young Daniel Defoe, who in 1707 published in his journal *Review* an elaborate case for recognizing Avery's kingdom: many ancient nations, Rome included, he observed, had been similarly founded by brigands of one sort or another; if the British government did not normalize relations with such a newly emerging power, it might well become a haven for enterprising criminals across the globe, and a danger to the empire. Shortly thereafter the enterprise was revealed to be a hoax. Nonetheless, works of popular fiction appeared, the first, a pamphlet in 1709 under the title *The Life and Adventures of Capt. John Avery; the Famous English Pirate, Now in Possession of Madagascar*, by Adrian van Broeck. Ten years later Defoe himself attempted to set the record straight with *The King of Pirates: Being an Account of the Famous Enterprises of Captain Avery, the Mock King of Madagascar with His Rambles and Piracies Wherein All the Sham Accounts Formerly Publish'd of Him, Are Detected* (1719). The Mughal princess was excised, and his utopian experiment eventually founders. A few years later, probably writing under the pseudonym of Captain Johnson in *A General History of the Pyrates* (1724), Defoe demotes Avery even further, making him an ineffective rascal who makes off with a heap of diamonds but dies in penury, whose crew descend into misery and Hobbesian chaos on the Malagasy mainland, and transfers the story of the great utopian experiment (now labeled Libertalia) to an entirely imaginary Captain Misson.

THE REAL ECONOMY OF SAINTE-MARIE

The actual history of Sainte-Marie might seem prosaic in comparison, but it was a genuine pirate settlement, and a place where those pillaging Indian Ocean shipping could easily find shelter and compatriots, and, at least between 1691 and 1699, dispose of some of their booty in exchange for some of the comforts of home. Several times a year, merchant ships would arrive from New York laden not just with ale, wine, spirits, gunpowder, and weapons, but with such essentials as woolens, mirrors, crockery, hammers, books, and sewing needles. They would return laden in part with pirate booty; in part, too, with Malagasy captives to be sold as slaves in Manhattan.

Ironically, it was the latter, the actual legal, "legitimate" commerce of Sainte-Marie, which almost led to the pirates' undoing.

The slave trade was nothing new in Madagascar. Arab merchants had been taking advantage of internal wars to extract captives since the Middle Ages. Still, during the early years of the European presence in the Indian Ocean, Madagascar's harbors were seen less as places to purchase slaves, than as for the resupply and refurbishment of ships heading back and forth from the cape. Gradually, the island developed something of a reputation in Europe as an exotic island paradise; tracts were published praising the virtues of its soils and climate, and both the French and British governments sponsored attempts at settler colonies: at Fort Dauphin in the southeast (1643–74), and St. Augustine Bay in the southwest (1644–46), respectively. Both failed. Dutch attempts to establish posts in the Bay of Antongil were similarly overwhelmed. In fact, one of the great mysteries about this period was that, while Madagascar had a long history of welcoming and incorporating merchants, settlers, and refugees from across the Indian Ocean region—not only from East Africa but from the Persian Gulf, Sri Lanka,

Sumatra, and other parts besides—European settlers were almost entirely unable to win a toehold.[6]

To some degree this was because would-be European settlers did, in fact, begin to get involved in the slave trade, which meant alliance with the most violent and unloved elements in Malagasy society, bandits or would-be warrior princes. But this can't be a full explanation, since many Arab merchants did the same, and were decidedly more successful. It was also because Malagasy had developed a set of expectations for how foreigners should behave, and Europeans were either unwilling or unable to abide by them. Somewhat different traditions had developed in this respect on the west and east coasts. In the west, commerce was dominated by Arab and Swahili merchants, called the Antalaotra or "Sea People," who formed their own port towns and remained in constant contact with their home communities. They tended to marry among themselves, but formed close alliances with Malagasy princes, who they supplied with magnificent luxuries, as well as weapons, in exchange for tropical products and slaves. The situation on the east coast was quite different. There the foreign presence seems to have been largely made up of political and religious refugees from across the Indian Ocean, who intermarried with the local population and became the core of new elites: sometimes new dynasties or aristocracies, sometimes magicians, curers, and intellectuals—and sometimes all of them.

European settlers in the sixteenth and seventeenth centuries did not pursue either strategy. They neither formed independent enclaves in alliance with Malagasy potentates, nor were they willing to intermarry and enter fully into the complex

games of aristocratic politics. In the first case, European traders were (especially in the beginning) not really in a position
to shower Malagasy allies with Oriental luxuries, because they
didn't really have access to Oriental luxuries to shower them
with; they were still largely interlopers in the ancient trading
world of the Indian Ocean, and their own countries' products
were not considered fit for kings. The one exception was firearms, but this only tended to reinforce the Malagasy impression
of Europeans as little more than violent savages. Over time, at
first the Dutch, and then the French and English, did manage
to supplant the Antalaotra as patrons of the Sakalava kings of
Boina and Menabe, but largely by muscling in on existing trade
networks in silks, porcelain, and magnificent luxuries by sheer
superior firepower. In other words, they were not unlike the pirates, and certainly that was how they were perceived by almost
everyone else in the region, for whom distinctions between pirates, slavers, colonists, and "legitimate traders" seemed so many
exotic legalistic niceties that had no effective bearing on how
those who appeared in a European ship were actually likely to
behave. Abbé Rochon notes European ships passing the island,

> which would, on more than one occasion, procure pro-
> visions by force, by visiting them with unexpected vex-
> ations, by burning their villages, or by terrorizing them
> with their artillery, if they were not quick enough in
> providing them with cattle, poultry, or rice. One can
> understand how after such violent acts, the sight of a
> European vessel would become for the islanders a pres-
> age of terror and calamity.[7]

At the same time, European racism ensured that those colonists who did attempt the second strategy were unable to fully integrate themselves into Malagasy society. The most telling anecdote in this regard relates to the final fate of the French colony at Fort Dauphin. The governors had, for the most part, been sensible enough to marry into important local families, and most of the colonists—almost all were men—had Malagasy wives and, before long, families. This, though, drew them into local politics, sparking behavior that even some French observers described as "atrocious cruelties."[8] Before long the surrounding population grew seethingly hostile, and their Malagasy kin afforded their only protection. Yet the moment French women appeared on the scene, they instantly abandoned those kin, with disastrous results:

> The colony's end came in 1674 when a shipload of young women bound for Bourbon (Réunion) was wrecked in the harbour. The women persuaded the governor to marry them to the colonists; the colonists' Malagasy wives then betrayed the colonists to the Malagasy forces, who massacred about 100 of them during the marriage festivities. The survivors soon left by ship, having spiked the cannon and burned the stores.[9]

Given this unfortunate history, to say that the pirates did better than previous European settlers at winning the acceptance of their Malagasy neighbors is perhaps not saying very much. But it also makes clear that the pirates had some real advantages over their compatriots. First of all, they actually did

have access to Oriental luxuries with which to regale local allies, and often in considerable quantities. Second, having so
absolutely rejected the social and political order of their home-
lands, they saw no reason not to fully integrate themselves. Before long, foreign observers began reporting Malagasy women
at the port of Sainte-Marie "wearing dresses of the most beautiful Indian materials embroidered in gold and silver, with golden
chains, bracelets, and even diamonds of considerable value."[10]
Baldridge himself married locally, and seems to have fathered
a number of children. Many pirates seem to have settled down
and become, effectively, Malagasy—or, to be more precise,
taken on the traditional role of half-Malagasy foreigners, "internal outsiders," one might call them, capable of mediating
with foreign traders, familiar in that part of the coast.

The path to this was not altogether smooth, however, and
here Baldridge's own fate is instructive. Since his operation
on Sainte-Marie was at least semilegal—for most of the 1690s
there was as yet no law against trading with outlaws—he was
under some of the same pressures from home that sparked some
of the worst behavior of earlier European traders. By his own
later account, he established a fort on the island and made it a
refuge for those fleeing from the endemic minor wars, raiding
and counterraiding, that characterized life on the mainland;
and then, with the help of the refugees, organized raids of
his own, to attain captives to trade for their captive relatives.
In the process, of course, some of those captives were sold to
the merchant ships regularly arriving from Manhattan. But
it would appear their numbers were never enough to satisfy
Philipse, back in New York. Baldridge's correspondence with

his patron, some of which has been preserved, is endlessly pep-
pered with indignant complaints about the small numbers and
inferior quality of the slaves he did manage to supply.

Despite the endless vituperations, large numbers of Malagasy slaves do appear to have ended up in the city. To get a
sense of how many: as late as 1741, when authorities in New
York uncovered what they believed to be a network of revolutionary cells planning an uprising in the city, they found them
to be organized by language—the most prominent being made
up of speakers of West African languages (Fante, Papa, and
Igbo), speakers of Irish, and speakers of Malagasy.[11]

Philipse stepped up the pressure even more as he learned
of the sugar plantations then being set up in Mauritius and
Réunion, which provided a ready nearby market. It's not clear
what he held over Baldridge's head, but it must have been
something serious, because by 1697, the old pirate was reduced
to an act of sheer self-destructive treachery: he lured several
dozen Malagasy allies, "men, women and children," onto a
merchant ship and sent them off in chains across the Atlantic.* When word got out, local lineage chiefs seem to have
decided the pirates had worn out their welcome, and a few
months later there was a coordinated attack on Sainte-Marie
and pirate settlements on the mainland. On Sainte-Marie the

---

* "Baldridge was the occasion of that Insurrection of the Natives and the
death of the pirates, for that having inveigled a great number of the natives of
St. Maries, men, women and children, on board a ship or ships he carryed and
sold them for slaves to a French Island called Mascarine or Mascaron, which
treachery of Baldridges the Natives on the Island revenged on those pirates by
cutting their throats" (Testimony of William Kidd, May 5, 1699, in Jameson,
ed., *Privateering and Piracy in the Colonial Period*, 187).

fortress was destroyed and about thirty pirates' throats cut—only a handful managed to escape to sea. The pirates seem to have gotten off more easily on the mainland, fending off their attackers (who might have just been trying to send a warning): in some cases they might have been tipped off, and in at least one—which seems to have been the major port town of Ambonavola, the later Foulpointe—because their Malagasy allies were willing to defend them.[12]

Baldridge was lucky. He was at sea on a voyage to Mauritius when the attacks took place, and, apprised of what happened, departed immediately for America. Six months later another commercial agent, one Edward Walsh, replaced him, and before long reports once again began to speak of a thriving town on the island, full of hundreds of freebooters. Still, the fortress was never rebuilt. The slave trade from Sainte-Marie ceased. But trade in booty became more difficult as well: the international notoriety of Avery, and later Captain Kidd (who had also been based on Sainte-Marie), eventually moved the authorities in London and New York to take more decisive action. The provisioning of criminals was made illegal, and they dispatched a largely symbolic punitive expedition (it failed to find any pirates). By that time, most of the pirates were living on the mainland, and their relations with their Malagasy hosts appear to have changed.[13]

THE REAL LIBERTALIA I: AMBONAVOLA

In 1697, then, the pirate settlers almost suffered the same fate as all previous European would-be settlers on the island. It was only the good relations the settlers on the mainland had with their Malagasy neighbors that allowed them to survive. Shifts in attitude toward slavers were particularly dramatic. Rather than participate, the pirates along the coast opposite Sainte-Marie ended up effectively defending the coast against the trade: since attacking or surreptitiously taking over slaving ships—often, with the connivance of the crews, who likewise turned pirate—became their principal way of acquiring new vessels. This, and fear of further rebellion, seems to have caused a profound change in the pirates' attitude toward conflict. Where men like Baldridge thrived on local unrest (which produced captives), and were notorious for stirring it up, the pirates, according to some of Captain Johnson's sources, gradually realized their interests were best served by doing the opposite.

In Johnson's *General History of the Pyrates*, the great hero of this later period, after the insurrection, is a man named Nathaniel North. North was a Bermudan who escaped having been pressed into the royal navy, and turned renegade in 1698. In the accounts he is always represented as a reluctant and unusually conscientious pirate. After a series of adventures and misadventures, he is reported to have found himself in command of a captured Indian ship that had been renamed the *Defiance* and armed with fifty-two cannons. After having lost its anchor at Fort Dauphin, the ship ended up drifting, on Christmas 1703, into a coastal bay called Ambonavola. It seems to have been a Malagasy town of some consequence, since several pirate accounts mention it as a stopping point for ships buying rice and other provisions, and some pirates had already tried to settle it, though they eventually gave the project up.* North seems to have decided it would be a good idea to try again. There were a dozen-odd members of the ship's original Indian crew still with them. One night, when the ship was left unguarded, North remarked to them that this might be an opportune moment for them to take back their vessel and sail home. They did so. The next day, when North's men realized what had happened, he chided them for their carelessness, and they good-naturedly shrugged the matter off and decided, after the Christmas revels were done, to make the best of the situation. Critically, they decided to maintain their existing organization on the land, and elected North the "captain" of their settlement. And so, according to Johnson:

> they endeavoured to make themselves easy, since there was no Help; and transporting their Goods to different Abodes, at small Distances, they settled themselves, buying Cattle and Slaves, and lived in a neighbourly Manner one among another five Years; clear'd a great deal of Ground, and planted Provisions as Yamms, Potatoes, &c.

---

* And more significantly, it's the only town in the region, other than Sainte-Marie, that they mention: so Baldridge notes the ship that first took him to Sainte-Marie in 1690 then stopped "in Bonnovolo on Madagascar, 16 leagues from St Maries" to buy rice (in Fox, *Pirates in Their Own Words*, 345); another pirate named Barrett testifies that after his crew took a Moorish ship and left it at Sainte-Marie in 1697, he went to live "at Madagascar at a place called Bonovolo, where he continued till Aprill 1698" (Fox, 70). So Ambonavola was already a major port of trade before the pirates arrived, and there were pirates settled there, too, by at least 1697, though it was briefly abandoned before being revived in 1703. All of this supports, but doesn't necessarily prove, that it was the same town that resisted the uprising of 1697, and was later known as Foulpointe.

The Natives among whom they fix'd, had frequent Broils and Wars among themselves, but the Pyrates interposed, and endeavoured to reconcile all differences; North deciding their Disputes not seldom, with that Impartiality and strict Regard to distributive Justice (for he was allowed, by all, a Man of admirable good natural Parts) that he ever sent away, even the Party who was cast, satisfy'd with the Reason, and content with the Equity of his Decisions.

What follows is no doubt an exaggerated and romanticized account, but there's nothing implausible about it. Sojourning foreigners of any sort frequently find themselves asked to mediate local disputes, and the description of pirate amity is rooted in historical fact—since, as outsiders frequently observed, pirates, despite being constantly armed and frequently drunk, virtually never came to blows with one another:

These Inclinations which the Pyrates shewed to Peace, and the Example they set of an amicable Way of Life; for they carefully avoided all Jars, and agreed to refer all Cause of Complaint among themselves which might arise, to a cool Hearing before North, and twelve of their Companions, gave them a great Character among the Natives, who were before very much prejudiced against the white Men. Nay, in this Point of keeping up a Harmony among themselves, they were so exact, that whoever spoke but in an angry or peevish Tone, was rebuked by all the Company, especially if before any of the

Country, tho' even but a Slave, of their own; for they thought, and very justly, that Unity and Concord were the only Means to warrant their Safety; for the People being ready to make War on one another upon the slightest Occasion, they did not doubt but they would take the Advantage of any Division which they might observe among the Whites, and cut them off whenever a fair Opportunity offered.

In other words, not only did they set themselves up as neutral mediators in local disputes, they studiously avoided any display of rancor internally, lest the Malagasy prey on their internal divisions in the same way men like Baldridge had preyed on theirs. The author (Johnson, who, again, is most likely Daniel Defoe) launches into detail about the improvised government that resulted:

On any Mistake from which a Dispute arose, or on any ill-manner'd Expression let fall in Company, they all broke up, and one of the Company poured what Liquor was before them on the Ground, saying, no Contention could creep in among them without Loss; and therefore he sacrificed that Liquor to the evil Fiend, to prevent a greater Damage. Then both the contending Parties, on Pain of being banished the Society, and sent to another Part of the Island, were summon'd to appear at Captain North's, the next Morning, and, in the mean while, they were commanded to keep their respective Houses.

The next Morning both the Parties being met, and

all the Whites summon'd to attend, the Captain set the Plaintiff and Defendant on one Side, and told them, that till the Agressor had consented to do Justice, and till the Person injured had forgot his Resentment, they must esteem them both Enemies to the Publick, and not look upon them as their Friends and Companions. He then wrote down the Names of all the Assembly, roll'd them up, and put them into a Hat, out of which, each Party shaking the Hat, chose six Tickets; and these twelve Rowls or Tickets contained the Names of the assistant Judges, who, with the Captain, heard and determined in the Cause, calling and examining the Witnesses.

All this was done in strict secret, lest any Malagasy realize that a dispute was taking place. The next day, according to the account, the matter was judged, with the inevitable punishment being the payment of some sort of fine: basically, a rearrangement of the pirate's individual stores of treasure.

The sacrifice to the devil might seem like it was made up for shock value, the author trying (as often) to provoke his bourgeois readers by suggesting even the most reprobate criminals were capable of better behavior than their own. But it might well be accurate, as, we'll see, descriptions of Malagasy ritual in the same chapter appear to be.*

Johnson goes on to describe how Ambonavola grew into a major pirate base, much like Sainte-Marie; how North and

---

* Though he's later described as favoring a Christian upbringing for his children (Johnson, *A General History*, 555).

his men formed alliances with nearby Malagasy "tribes," as well as monarchs farther to the north and south of the island; how they became embroiled in a variety of local conflicts; how North married and had three Malagasy children. After a brief return to marauding in 1707, North retired permanently, though he was eventually—perhaps sometime around 1712, no one is quite sure—killed in his bed by a party of Malagasy taking revenge for some earlier conflict.

Most of these details are known only from the *General History* and other popular authors writing at the time; there has been surprisingly little work by historians of Madagascar on who the various Malagasy parties named in the text might actually have been, and how to integrate these events into larger Malagasy history. It's not even absolutely certain where Ambonavola was; but since it is said to have been located some thirty miles south of Sainte-Marie, and to have been a large and enduring settlement, it would pretty much have to have been either the later Fenoarivo or Foulpointe, and Molet-Sauvaget[14] makes a convincing case that it was the latter.* But it's easy to see how the new pirate role, of establishing themselves largely as peaceful mediators, combining their wealth and finery with a sense of social justice, might have contributed to the utopian fantasies that were already circu-

---

* Molet-Sauvaget suggests that the pirates referred to the location as "Ambonavola point," which became "Bonavola point" (pronounced "Boonavool"), and then by a play of words, "Fool's Point." When the language of trade became French, this came to be rendered "Foulpointe." Compare Allibert, *Histoire de la Grande Isle Madagascar*, 471n11. I should note that if Allibert is right and Ambonavola is not Foulpointe but the nearby Fenerive, it wouldn't actually make a great deal of difference for the argument.

lating around the figure of Avery. The pirates, in Johnson's narrative, were treated as princes by their neighbors. But in fact they seem to have been assiduous in converting the democratic institutions first developed on board ships into forms that would be viable on land. And as we shall see, there is good reason to believe their Malagasy neighbors were indeed influenced by their example.

MORE MOCK KINGS: JOHN PLANTAIN

To write a definitive history of the pirate implantation in Madagascar is quite impossible. The sources are meager, they consist of little more than narratives written at the time for popular audiences and a handful of court documents, including often laconic accounts of those later arrested for piracy in England or America. When several accounts of the same event exist, they usually contradict one another. The popular accounts are often overtly sensationalistic—however, this does not mean they aren't true, since clearly a fair number of quite sensational things did happen. Surprisingly little research has been conducted on the Malagasy side. All we have, then, are a series of tiny windows on extraordinary events.

Still, the basic facts are not in question. Buccaneers continued to make the "pirate round" via Madagascar until roughly 1722, when the British and French governments began seriously cracking down on raiding. Some merely passed through, and retired in Réunion, where the governor was willing to accept a share of booty to grant pirates clemency.

Some became advisors to the Sakalava kings, others assistants to Abraham Samuel, a pirate who was—through some local machinations—temporarily placed on the throne of the former Matitana kingdom near the abandoned French settlement of Fort Dauphin. But most of those who stayed preferred to remain in the northeast, either creating settlements of their own like North, or moving in with their Malagasy families.

Of those who formed pirate communities, some did declare themselves kings and made grandiose claims, sometimes to sovereignty over the entire island, presenting their wives as local princesses. The best known today is John Plantain, "the King of Ranter Bay," since his story was extensively written up by an East India Company agent named Clement Downing, whose book, *A Compendious History of the Indian Wars* (1737), contains a fairly long digression about Madagascar. Downing met Plantain in 1722; he describes him at that time as the very image of the swashbuckler, greeting him on the beach in rough clothes with two pistols stuck in his breeches:

> Plantain, James Adair, and Hans Burgen, the Dane, had fortified themselves very strongly at Ranter-Bay; and taken possession of a large Tract of Country. Plantain having the most Money of them all, called himself King of Ranter-Bay, and the Natives commonly sing Songs in praise of Plantain. He brought great Numbers of the Inhabitants to be subject to him, and seem'd to govern them arbitrarily; tho' he paid his Soldiers very much to their Satisfaction . . .
>
> Plantain's House was built in as commodious a man-

ner as the Nature of the Place would admit; and for
his further State and Recreation, he took a great many
Wives and Servants, whom he kept in great Subjection;
and after the English manner, called them Moll, Kate,
Sue or Pegg. These Women were dressed in the richest
Silks, and some of them had Diamond Necklaces. He fre-
quently came over from his own Territories to St. Mary's
Island, and there began to repair several Parts of Capt.
Avery's Fortifications.[15]

Plantain established himself in Madagascar at just the
time the legend of Henry Avery was at its peak, and agents
of the imaginary pirate government were traveling from court
to court in Europe, seeking alliances. Hence the reference to
"Avery's Fortifications," which is, of course, really Adam
Baldridge's old fort in Sainte-Marie harbor, destroyed in the insurrection of 1697. Plantain seems to have done everything he
could to play on the legend.* While Downing's descriptions are
superficially credible, just about everything in the story smacks
of tall tales designed to impress gullible foreigners. (One of the

---

* Plantain, at least, did actually exist (see testimony of Richard Moor, who
met him in 1720, in Fox, *Pirates in Their Own Words*, 212); Downing is generally a fairly credible, if imperfect, witness to things he saw himself (Risso,
"Cross-Cultural Perceptions of Piracy"). Deschamps (*Les pirates à Madagascar*,
175) suggests Plantain was confused by the title *mpanjaka*, given to him by the
villagers, which could refer to almost anyone with administrative power, and
actually imagined himself a king. A more plausible reading is that he began by
trying to impress Commodore Downing, who was after all sent on an expedition to root out pirates, and, finding he seemed to believe every tall tale he told
him, ended up trying to see just how ridiculous a lie he could get away with.

most colorful details of Downing's account is the Malagasy choruses singing songs of praise of his conquests—"and at the end of almost every Verse was pronounced, Plantain King of Ranter-Bay; which he seemed mightily pleas'd with, as well as with Dances perform'd by the great Bodies of the Natives."[16] Since Downing did not speak Malagasy, we of course have no way to know what the lyrics actually were.)

Downing also describes meeting with the commander of Plantain's Malagasy troops, a man he calls "Molatto Tom," or simply "the young Captain Avery," since he claimed to be the son of the legendary pirate himself:

This Molatto Tom was one that was so much fear'd amongst them, that at the very sight of him, they would seem to tremble. They often would have made him a King, but he never would take that Title upon him. He was a Man of tall Stature, very clean-limb'd, and of a pleasant Countenance . . . He had long black Hair like the Malabar or Bengal Indians; which made me think he might be the Son of Capt. Avery, got on some of the Indian Women he took in the Moors ship, which had the Grand Mogul's Daughter on board. This is very proba-ble; for he said he could not remember his Mother . . . till he was told his Mother died when he was an Infant.[17]

Again, since Avery did not really return to Madagascar with any Indian princesses, this can only be pure fantasy; but it also seems clear his hosts were having a good deal of fun with him, vying to see exactly how much they could put over on the naive Englishman. Downing duly recorded everything they told him, how Plantain got himself into a war with the Sakalava king Toakafo ("who the Pyrates called Long Dick, or King Dick")[18] after he was refused the king's granddaughter's hand in marriage; how this led to a complicated and increasingly unlikely set of campaigns where Plantain's army marched back and forth across the island, their left flank bearing a Scottish flag and the right flank a Danish one; and how, after much carnage, ingenious ploys, and horrific executions, they ended up in possession of the ports of Masselage, St. Augustine, Fort Dauphin, and all points in between. Plantain now ruled the entire island of Madagascar.

In fact, by the time the account is over, Downing has even largely contradicted his own initial description, since he notes that after his victories Plantain did indeed settle down with King Dick's granddaughter, named Eleanor Brown after her English father, a devoted Christian who he loved dearly even though when he married her she was already pregnant with another man's child. Rather than lording it over his wives and servants, he

gave her the whole Government of his Household Affairs, discharging several of his other Women . . . He cloth'd her with the richest Jewels and Diamonds he had, and gave her twenty Girl Slaves to wait on her. It was this Woman that Mr. Christopher Lisle would have been great with; for which Attempt Plantain shot him dead on the spot.[19]

The story ends with additional seaman's scuttlebutt, gathered some years later. One doesn't need to read between the lines very much to figure out what must have happened. After having declared himself "The Great King of Madagascar," and selling off a large number of captives to passing British ships, Plantain came to realize his position was as untenable as Baldridge's had been, and—perhaps warned by his "general" Tom that he would likely soon meet the same fate—evacuated Ranter Bay with his wife and children for greener pastures in India.

SOME PROBLEMS WITH CHRONOLOGY

The most remarkable thing about Downing's account of John Plantain is the date the encounter took place: 1722. The character he describes as "Mulatto Tom" is clearly Ratsimilaho. Now, Ratsimilaho was indeed the son of an English pirate, and was known to foreigners as "Tom Tsimilaho" or sometimes just "Tom." The pirates' Malagasy children were then known as "Malata," which is derived from the English "mulatto." So it is extremely unlikely "Mulatto Tom" could have been anyone else. But this makes the story he and Plantain were telling Downing all the more mischievous, since by 1722 it was certainly Ratsimilaho, and not the pirate, who was actually king of the northeast coast.

According to the now generally accepted historical account, the period between the years 1712 and 1720 had seen a prolonged series of wars in the northeast between the armies of two rival confederations—the Betsimisaraka, commanded by Ratsimilaho, and the Tsikoa or Betanimena, commanded by a military leader named Ramangano, who had seized control of the ports of the coast.* These wars culminated in the absolute victory of the Betsimisaraka. But if this is true, then Ratsimilaho would have already been the uncontested ruler of the northeast coast for two years when he met Downing, and decided, for some reason (possibly, just for his own amusement) to pretend to be a mere general to a Jamaican adventurer.

So what sort of king goes about pretending to be a mere general?

Our main source for Ratsimilaho's life is a narrative written in 1806 by a French author named Nicolas Mayeur, who based his account on interviews with the king's old companions made while he was living in Tamatave, then the Betsimisaraka kingdom's capital, between 1762 and 1767.[20] While the narrative provides a highly romanticized account of Ratsimilaho's life, it's quite long and detailed and, understandably, has become the basis of the standard textbook version of Malagasy history of the epoch. Yet this standard account is extremely difficult to square with contemporary ones like Downing's.

Even the circumstances that led Mayeur to conduct his researches is revealing of the topsy-turvy circus-mirror world of extravagant imperial claims characteristic of the region—indeed, still characteristic of the region a century later. May-

---

* The dates were first proposed by Nicolas Mayeur ("Histoire de Ratsimilaho") and confirmed by Grandidier (*Les habitants de Madagascar*, 184n2).

eur was a French slave trader and adventurer, who'd grown up in Madagascar and spoke fluent Malagasy. At the time he conducted his research on Ratsimilaho, he was being employed as a spy by one Maurice-Auguste Count de Benyowsky, a Polish aristocrat who, having escaped from prison in Siberia and made his way to France, managed to convince Louis XV to put him in charge of a project to conquer Madagascar. Count Benyowsky established himself in a village (which he renamed "Louisville") in the Bay of Antongil, not far from Rantabe, and began requisitioning supplies from France in support of his conquests, which he documented with regular letters back to court. For instance, in September 1774, he reported that with a force of a mere 160 active soldiers, he'd managed to secure a kingdom of thirty-two provinces paying tribute of almost four million francs, and comprising almost the entirety of the island.[21] These reports were, needless to say, pure fantasy. In fact, what evidence we have indicates Benyowsky was not really a Polish count at all, but a Hungarian con man, who used the provisions sent from France to pay off the surrounding villagers into playing along with the pretense he was king, and then spent most of his time gallivanting about the world passing himself off as King of Madagascar. (In 1777, for instance, he was a frequent chess partner of Benjamin Franklin's in Paris; in 1779, he was in America, offering to put his kingdom at the disposal of the revolution.)

The problem was that since Benyowsky had virtually no idea what was really going on in Madagascar, he frequently came under suspicion by royal authorities. At least one commission of inquiry was sent out, though the "count" seems to have used his influence to have the results suppressed. In order to make his reports more realistic, Benyowsky began paying Mayeur, then operating as a slave trader, to write detailed reports on political conditions around the island.[22] Mayeur did so, and numerous accounts of his travels have survived, providing precious historical insights into conditions at the time. So the first real ethnographic accounts we have of Madagascar are really notes written by a spy in order to allow a con man to better fabricate accounts of his nonexistent exploits. While employed by Benyowsky, Mayeur became fascinated with the story of the origin of the Betsimisaraka Confederation, and the heroic figure of Ratsimilaho, and appears to have interviewed all surviving eyewitnesses to the wars of 1712–20 that he could find, including some of the king's early close companions. In Mayeur's later retirement on the island of Réunion, around 1806, a bookish local named Froberville convinced him to write up the results in the form of a handwritten book, entitled *Histoire de Ratsimila-hoe Roi de Foule-pointe et des Bétsi-miçaracs*, which documents, over the course of 120 very large handwritten pages (replete with Froberville's own scholarly footnotes), the story of Ratsimilaho's life.

The manuscript remains unpublished; most scholars have, for the last century or so, relied on summaries.[23] Still, Mayeur's version of events has become canonical. According to Mayeur, Ratsimilaho's father, Tom, first tried to send his son to England for an education, but the boy quickly fell homesick and demanded to be brought back; his father then gave him a stock of muskets and ammunition and left him to find his fortune. At the time, the territory around Foulpointe was under the control of a tyrannical ruler named Ramangano, head of the Tsikoa Confederation, based in the south. Ratsimilaho raised a rebellion, and most of the manuscript's twenty-four chapters are taken up with the details of the resulting war, which lasted eight years, and entailed thousands of casualties. Over the course of the conflict, Ratsimilaho managed—in Mayeur's glowing account, largely due to his own personal brilliance and charisma—to create a new political entity, called the Betsimisaraka ("the many unsundered"), which, after his final victory in 1720, united the entire northeast under a single government. Over the course of these wars, Ratsimilaho himself was first elected temporary supreme leader, then permanent king, under the title Ramaromanompo ("He who renders many servants"). In the end, Ratsimilaho unified the entire northeast under a single enlightened monarchy, married a daughter of the Sakalava king (named Matavy, or "Fat"), sired an heir (named Zanahary, or "God"), and finally, after a long and successful reign, died at the age of fifty-six, in 1750.

Ratsimilaho would appear to be the only character in this hall of mirrors who actually was a genuine king. What's more, over the course of his reign, the king's fellow Zana-Malata gradually managed to establish themselves as a self-identified, intermarrying aristocracy, and remained so for at least the next century. Over the second half of the eighteenth century, however, they fell to squabbling, manipulated by French slave traders based on the plantation islands of Mauritius and Réunion; Ratsimilaho's successors (Zanahary, 1750–67; Iavy, 1767–91; Zakavola, 1791–1803) proved unable to control the situation, and the kingdom fell apart. The general consensus of historians is that Ratsimilaho's project ultimately failed. According to some,[24] this was because he did not give it a proper ritual basis to become a full-fledged Malagasy dynasty like the Sakalava; according to others,[25] because the pressure of the demand for slaves from the newly emerging plantation economies of Mauritius and Réunion—only just beginning in the time of the pirates—was ultimately overwhelming. Before long, corrupted leaders were concocting reasons for wars or even attacking their own villages to acquire captives with which to pay their debts to French slave traders. In the end, the kingdom fractured into a disorganized collection of warring polities that were then easily absorbed by the armies of Radama I in 1817. Tamatave became the Merina kingdom's second city, and gateway to the capital, as it remains today. The rest of the Betsimisaraka country soon took on the complexion it did in the colonial period, alternating between territories dominated by foreign-owned plantations, producing cloves, vanilla, and coffee for the world market, and rural backwaters, their inhabitants notorious for their resistance to any form of centralized authority.

All of this is standard fare in Malagasy history books. In most such histories, the pirates form one chapter, their children, another. By the time the war between Ratsimilaho and Ramangano begins, the torch is assumed to have been passed to a new generation. But if one examines a simple time line of events (see Appendix), it's clear that the conventional view cannot possibly be right.

First, if the war for the creation of the Betsimisaraka Confederation really did last from 1712 to 1720, as Mayeur asserts, and subsequent historians have accepted, then the pirate set-tlements at Sainte-Marie and Ambonavola would have still been active at the time. Second, it's very difficult to imagine how one could really attribute the pirate's children much of a role in the creation of the confederation in 1712, since while Ratsimilaho himself was said to have been eighteen years of age at the time, he was obviously an exceptional character; of the other Malata, none could possibly have been older than twenty-one, and the vast majority must have been children living with their parents in those very settlements. And in-deed in Mayeur's account, the Malata themselves play almost no role in the unfolding of events.

We are dealing, then, with political institutions that were created by Malagasy political actors, living in close contact with active pirates. In Mayeur's account "the whites" never ap-pear as individuals, but remain at best a kind of ghostly pres-ence at the fringes. But in fact they were almost certainly at least indirectly involved in the course of events.

Finally, foreign observers at the time cast Ratsimilaho in a strange confusion of roles. He is said to have begun his wars of liberation in 1712. Yet in the middle of the war, in 1715, Dutch merchants report someone of the same name ("Tom Tsimilaho") as chief minister to the Sakalava king Toakafo of Boina—the "Long Dick" of Plantain's story. A year later he is a local chief in Antongil, and coming to the aid of some shipwrecked Europeans from Réunion; but then in 1722, we have both de la Galaisière claiming he is king of the entire northeast, and Clement Downing, who finds him pretend-ing to be the mere commander of the forces of a self-declared pirate sovereign at Rantabe. Eleven years later, some French observers are under the impression he was merely one chief among many in that region. Others duly report that he is, in fact, the king of the entire east coast.

No doubt at least some of these observers were simply confused; but it's clear that at least in some cases their Malagasy and European informants were doing their best to keep them that way. For instance, in 1733, Charpentier de Cossigny, an engineer in the employ of the French East India Company on a mission to the Bay of Antongil, met a certain "King Baldridge" there: presumably, son of the famous pirate king of Sainte-Marie. Baldridge insisted that there were two other kings in the region, "Thame Tsimalau," and an otherwise unknown De La Ray. Cossigny observed that unlike Baldridge, who was an amenable fellow, Ratsimilaho seemed of a difficult and unpleasant character.

What is one to make of this? Did Ratsimilaho really just control part of this particular territory? Or was Baldridge just putting on airs, and Ratsimilaho reacting with irritation at his pretensions? (And was "Baldridge" *really* a descendant of Adam Baldridge's? Or was he lying about that as well?)

It's hard to say anything for certain, but if nothing else, we are clearly dealing with a profoundly different notion of sovereignty than that familiar from most of Eurasia at the time. A provincial governor under Henry VIII, or Suleiman the Magnificent, who put on such airs would have found his head on a platter very swiftly. In fact, one reason I suspect that everything seemed so negotiable was that none of these kingdoms had much of a social base—that is, other than the ability to summon up a few hundred, or in emergencies perhaps a few thousand, warriors. It would seem that aside from the Sakalava kings out west, who had reshaped the local landscape, cutting down forests, turning farmland into pasture for their vast herds of cattle, and thus completely reconfiguring social relations among their subjects, most Malagasy "kings" of this period existed in a kind of predatory bubble, full of magnificent finery, but lacking any real ability to interfere systematically in the daily lives of those they claimed as subjects.

The world of course has long been full of petty bandit kings making grandiose claims, but the peculiar situation of northeast Madagascar in the seventeenth and eighteenth centuries made this an unusually easy game to play. The existence of vast amounts of pirate booty gave such men the ability to perform all the external trappings of a royal court—the gold and jewels, the harems, the synchronized dance routines— even in the complete absence of the means to mobilize any significant amount of human labor outside their own home settlements. Merina or Sakalava kings, for instance, could summon representatives of every ancestry in their kingdoms to construct their houses or tombs or to attend royal rituals. There is no reason at all to believe that (either) Baldridge, or North, or Plantain, or Benyowsky, or even Ratsimilaho could do anything of the sort—or even, that any of them really aspired to. There is certainly no evidence that even at the height of his power, Ratsimilaho presided over anything remotely like what we might consider a state.

There is one profound difference, however, between Ratsimilaho's case and all the others. The rise of the Betsimisaraka Confederation did affect the larger society in profound ways—just, it was in almost exactly the opposite of the ways one would have imagined the creation of a kingdom would have done. When the pirates arrived in Madagascar in the late seventeenth century, they encountered a society marked by constant internal warfare, dominated by something very like a priestly caste, and an emerging warrior elite that was already beginning to sort itself into a system of hierarchical ranks. This society had communal elements, but could not really be called in any sense egalitarian. Society under Ratsimilaho, in contrast, seems to have been in many respects more egalitarian than what had come before.

The arrival of the pirates sparked a chain of reactions—first the commercial self-assertion of Malagasy women, then a political reaction to that by young men—for which Ratsimilaho became, effectively, the figurehead, which ultimately created Betsimisaraka society as it exists today. Let us turn, then, to consider how things looked from the Malagasy point of view.

PART II

THE ADVENT OF THE PIRATES FROM A MALAGASY POINT OF VIEW

A SEXUAL REVOLUTION AGAINST
THE CHILDREN OF ABRAHAM?

An Enchantress, living in one of the islands of the Indian Archipelago, saves the life of a Pirate, a man of savage but noble nature.

—from Mary Shelley's notes
on her late husband's unfinished writing projects

WHILE THE PIRATES USED MADAGASCAR AS A BASE TO RAID the Red Sea and across the Indian Ocean at least as far as Malacca, people had been moving in the opposite direction for many centuries before. The medieval history of the east coast of Madagascar in particular appears to have been marked by the periodic appearance of new waves of immigrants, most claiming Muslim origins, who established themselves as ritual, mercantile, or political aristocracies, or often all three at once. In the southeast for instance, the Zafiraminia, who seem to have their origins in Java or Sumatra, based their power in part on expertise of command of an astrological system rooted in the Arabic lunar calendar—and established a monopoly over the slaughter of cattle. This both ensured their supervision of any major ritual event, and allowed them to dominate the emerging cattle trade to supply the merchantmen who began stopping off in Madagascar for provisioning from at least the sixteenth century. Paul Ottino[1] has argued, sometimes convincingly, that the Raminia were originally mystically oriented Shiite refugees—their eponymous ancestor was said to have been created by God from the foam of the sea, and married to Fatima, the sister of the Prophet. Their grandiose cosmological claims were seen as so peculiar by the first Portuguese observers that they hesitated to call them Muslims at all, and over the period from 1509 to 1513, these same Portuguese noted the appearance of a new wave of East African Sunnis landing in the region, founders of the rival Antemoro kingdom, who set about to exterminate them as heretics. Over time, the Antemoro managed to establish themselves as the quintessential intellectuals and astrologers of Madagascar, preserving their knowledge in books in Arabic script called *sorabe*; the Raminia, in turn, scattered, eventually becoming the ancestors of a series of southern dynasties, including, most significantly, the Zafimbolamena lineage that founded the Sakalava kingdoms of Boina and Menabe.[2]

These migrations have been endlessly discussed and debated. Less noted is the fact that there appears to have been a regular clash between the patriarchal sensibilities of the various newcomers and the relatively relaxed sexual mores of their Malagasy subjects and neighbors. Antemoro histories, for instance, complain of natives who traced descent through women,* and part of Antemoro strategy in wiping out the Zafiraminia was to kill adult males, and sequester captive women to ensure they produced pious children.[3] Even in the nineteenth century, the Antemoro were famous for insisting on premarital virginity, among a larger population for whom the sexual freedom of adolescents of both sexes is simply assumed as a matter of course. Any unmarried girl who became pregnant, and could not prove the father of her child was a Muslim of the correct ancestry, would be stoned or drowned.[4] Boys, in contrast, could carry on as they pleased. According to local traditions, it was precisely these sexual restrictions that most rankled the population, and were the direct cause of the nineteenth-century uprising that put an end to the kingdom.

Paul Ottino[5] has made something of a career of attempting to trace back the origins of Malagasy myth to different strands of Arab, Persian, Indian, and African philosophy. It's often hard to know exactly what to make of these arguments, but one thing is clear: frequent visitors from other parts of the Indian Ocean, and periodic infusions of new migrants, ensured that the island was in no sense isolated from the rest of the world, its intellectual currents included. At the same time, these various strains of foreign intruders were ultimately, with very few exceptions, absorbed into the larger Malagasy cultural grid. Within a few generations, newcomers had forgotten their original languages and most distinctive cultural traits (by the seventeenth century, for instance, even the Antemoro were no longer familiar with the Koran), but

---

* They presumably meant not matrilineally, but cognatically.

instead adopted some variation on a fairly standard repertoire of pan-Malagasy customs, from oratory to rice cultivation to elaborate circumcision and mortuary ritual. Since the immigrants were largely, if not exclusively, male, Malagasy women obviously played a central role in all this, and one can see attempts by various immigrant elites to sequester and control women, and particularly to control their sexuality, as efforts to maintain their own cultural distinctiveness and, thus, elite status, for as long as possible. (All failed in the end, since all have by now vanished as independent groups.)

Were similar dynamics happening in the northeast? They were; but with one peculiar twist. The local alien aristocracy in what was later to become Betsimisaraka territory did not claim to be Muslim, but Jewish.

Here is what Étienne de Flacourt, the governor of the ill-fated French colony at Fort Dauphin, had to say about them in his *Histoire de la Grande Isle de Madagascar* in 1661:

Those who I believe to have come the first are the Zafi-Ibrahim, or of the line of Abraham, who live on the isle of St. Mary and nearby territories, especially as, having the custom of circumcision, they have no trace of Mohammedism, are not familiar with Mohammed or the Caliphs, and consider their followers as Kafirs and lawless men; they do not eat with or contract any alliances with them. They celebrate and refrain from work on Saturday, not Friday like the Moors, and do not have any names similar to those they use, which makes me believe that their ancestors came to this island during the earliest migrations of the Jews, or that they are de-scended from the oldest families of Ishmaelites from before the Babylonian captivity or those that remained in Egypt after the exodus of the children of Israel: they have retained the names of Moses, of Isaac, of Jacob and of Noah. Some of them, perhaps, have come from the shores of Ethiopia.[6]*

Elsewhere he adds that the Zafy Ibrahim dominated the coast from Antongil to Tamatave, and maintained a monopoly on animal sacrifice similar to the Zafiraminia; that on Sainte-Marie itself there were five or six hundred of them in twelve villages, all under a chief named "Raignasse or Raniassa the son of Rasiminon,"[7] who collected a tenth of their fishing and harvests.

Numerous scholars have speculated on the origins and identity of the Zafy Ibrahim (also referred to as the Zafi-Hibrahim, Zafi-Boraha, or Zafi-Borahy—the island is known in Malagasy as Nosy Borahy today). Grandidier[8] thought they

---

* *Ceux que j'estime être venus les premiers, ce sont les Zafe-Ibrahim ou de la lignée d'Abraham, qui habitent l'isle de Sainte-Marie et les terres voisines, d'autant que, ayant usage de la circoncision, ils n'ont aucune tâche du Mahométisme, ne connaissent Mahomet ni ses califes, et réputent ses sectateurs pour Cafres et hommes sans loi, ne mangent point et ne contractent aucune alliance avec eux. Ils célèbrent et chôment le samedi, non le vendredi comme les Mores, et n'ont aucun nom semblable à ceux qu'ils portent, ce qui me 'fait croire que leurs ancêtres sont passés en cette isle dès les premières transmigrations des Juifs ou qu'ils sont descendus des plus anciennes familles des Ismaélites dès avant la captivité de Babylone ou de ceux qui pouvaient être restés dans l'Egypte environ la sortie des enfants d'Israël: ils ont retenu le nom de Moïse, d'Isaac, de Joseph, de Jacob et de Noé. Il en est peut-être venu quelques-uns des côtes d'Ethiopie.*

were, indeed, Yemeni Jews; Ferrand[9] suggested Kharijites; Ottino[10] Qarmatians, or perhaps Coptic or Nestorian Christians; and Allibert[11] has more recently speculated they might be the descendants of pre-Islamic Arabs, who sojourned in Ethiopia before making their way south. Anything is possible. Still, most of those who object to seeing the Zafy Ibrahim as Jewish assume that Flacourt's account is our only evidence, and that the governor was simply confused. This does not seem to be true. As late as the nineteenth century, one English missionary reported meeting representatives of the Zafy Ibrahim farther south who insisted that "we are altogether Jews."[12] I see no reason not to defer to his informants' opinions on this matter.

By the colonial period, the Zafy Ibrahim were confined to Sainte-Marie (still known in Malagasy as Nosy Boraha, or the Island of Abraham) and, increasingly, had come to see themselves primarily as Arabs;* those on the mainland had long since been absorbed into the larger body of the Betsimisaraka. In Flacourt's time, however, they seem to have filled much the same role as the Zafiraminia in the south, living in scattered communities on the mainland, with a monopoly on the slaughter of livestock (for which they performed a special prayer, known as *mivorika*,† though Flacourt says they rendered no other cult to their high God), and also as merchants,

---

* Here Ferrand provides a convincing case (1905, 411–15). This was confirmed by my own informants from Sainte-Marie, who insisted they were "Arabs."
† A curious term since *mivorika* means to bewitch or ensorcel in contemporary Malagasy, but apparently in ancient texts it was used for "prayer" (Allibert, *Histoire de la Grande Isle Madagascar*, 470–71). If the word specifically referred to Zafy Ibrahim ritual, it's quite possible that it changed meaning when the group fell out of favor.

as the fact that they positioned themselves on Sainte-Marie, a frequent stopping point for foreign merchants, strongly suggests.

A case could also be made that the Zafy Ibrahim did leave their mark on the Betsimisaraka, into whom they were subsequently absorbed. Of all the peoples of Madagascar, the Betsimisaraka are known, not just for their egalitarianism and resistance to centralized authority, but also for their penchant for philosophical and cosmological speculation.[13] This speculation tends to take a relentlessly dualistic character often quite different in tone than that found in other parts of Madagascar. In Betsimisaraka myths, there is a constant emphasis on the creation of the universe, and of humanity in particular, by two counterposed forces: a God of Above and a God of Below. Cosmogonic stories describe how the terrestrial god created figures of humans and animals, of wood or clay, but was unable to animate them; the sky god blows life into them, but, usually because of some broken promise or unpaid debt, ultimately returns to take it away again; hence as it's often put, "God kills us," and our bodies return to the earth.* It was this dualism, in turn, that seems to have inspired early

---

* Such themes are not unknown elsewhere in Madagascar, but if one surveys Haring's comprehensive Malagasy folktale index (*Malagasy tale index*), definite patterns immediately jump out. Most dramatically, the Zatovo cycle (Lombard, "Zatovo qui n'a pas été créé par Dieu"; cf. Graeber, "Culture as Creative Refusal"), perhaps the quintessential Malagasy myth about a young upstart who claims not to be created by God, is entirely absent among the Betsimisaraka, though it's present in one form or another just about everywhere else. In those stories, features of human life are represented as being, essentially, stolen from a Jovian high God. The Betsimisaraka stories instead represent the situation as a result not of Promethean rebellion, but of a balance between two cosmic forces.

European observers to compare the Malagasy of the northeast to Manichaeans[14]—evidence from early travelers' accounts suggests that this attitude might have once been much more common, with Malagasy informants explaining that while they recognize the existence of a distant high God, who ultimately gives and takes their lives, they render him no cult, but instead direct their prayers and sacrifices toward terrestrial powers responsible for their more immediate misfortunes, who the European observers invariably referred to as "the devil." Such accounts inspired Paul Ottino[15] to suggest the Zafy Ibrahim might have been outright Gnostics, perhaps of Qarmatian or other Ismaili origin.* This seems unlikely, though, again, some kind of Gnostic influence is not impossible.

One thing that is clear is that the Zafy Ibrahim were in their heyday notorious—like the Muslim communities that also existed on the northeast coast—for their jealous posses-

---

* Here Ottino does appear to be overstating his case. The passage from Rochon actually refers to Islamic immigrants who he says have been absorbed into the Malagasy population to the point of having lost most of the tenets of their religion; similar statements, that Malagasy recognize but do not render cult to a benevolent high God, but rather to "the devil," can be found in numerous accounts of the island, and not just to migrant populations. Mayeur, for instance, describes a Betsimisaraka sacrifice around 1716 thus: "When the body was placed on the earth, he sacrificed five oxen, of which one part was brought to the deceased, one destined for the devil, the other to God. The rest was distributed to those attending, who ate it in common" ("Histoire de Ratsimilaho," 210). Similarly, Ottino's argument ("Le Moyen-Age") that a strain of Qarmatian "communism" can be traced in Flacourt's description of the Zafy Ibrahim as having neither rich nor poor, treating their slaves like children, and marrying them to their daughters (*Histoire de la Grande Isle*, 23) seems to rest on a slippage in Flacourt's description, from the Zafy Ibrahim as ritual specialists on the east coast, to a description of the manner of life of the east coast population in general.

siveness toward their wives and daughters. Charles Dellon, who published an account of the region in 1669, insists that the Middle Eastern immigrants in Antongil and Fenerive ("Galamboule") were quite exceptional in this regard:

> Marriage has no rules among some peoples of Madagascar; they marry one another without demanding reciprocal promises and leave each other when they wish; the method is entirely different in the country of Galamboule and Antongil; they guard their wives, who are in no sense in common, and death is imposed on those who are surprised in some infidelity.[16]

Elsewhere Dellon describes the same people as lapsed Muslims, whose faith is now largely reduced to refraining from pork and the fact that unlike their neighbors they are jealous "to the point of fury," putting "libertines" to death.[17] Another source speaks of crowds of men from villages on Sainte-Marie attacking Dutch sailors for flirting with local women,[18] and Flacourt confirms that much unlike other Malagasy, the wives and daughters of the Zafy Ibrahim were "as difficult of access as our own daughters of France, as their fathers and mothers guarded them most carefully."[19]

As in the case of the Antemoro, all of this was no doubt part of a strategy of social reproduction, a way of maintaining the group's status as a group of internal outsiders—foreigners from the perspective of ordinary Malagasy, Malagasy from the perspective of actual foreigners. It was a strategy that could be maintained only by a good deal of violence and threats of violence, primarily against the group's own womenfolk. One can get a glimpse, perhaps, of the sense the Zafy Ibrahim must have had of the dangers of being absorbed by the surrounding population by a myth that was still being told in the late nineteenth century of how they first came to Nosy Boraha (the island of Sainte-Marie). Their ancestor Boraha, they claimed, was a shipwrecked fisherman whose crew found themselves on an island inhabited entirely by women. The natives killed his companions, but one merciful old woman kept Boraha hidden by day in a great chest, allowing him out at night to fish. One evening, he encountered a dolphin who agreed to carry him on its back to safety, and it conducted him to Nosy Boraha.[20]*

As Alfred Grandidier[21] observed, all these seventeenth-century accounts of sequestered women referred to the descendants of Middle Eastern immigrants—some Muslim, some Jewish—all of whom have, indeed, since been absorbed into the larger population. He notes such descriptions abruptly end around the time the pirates appear on the scene in the 1690s, and that in subsequent times, even on Sainte-Marie itself, there was no longer anything to distinguish the sexual mores of the inhabitants from those of any other Malagasy. As elsewhere in Madagascar, premarital adventures came to be considered a normal part of growing up, sex outside of marriage a peccadillo at best, but "furious" jealousy on the part of either spouse a profound moral flaw.

---

* I don't ordinarily go in for this sort of thing but the myth veritably screams for a Freudian interpretation: surrounded by the dangerous sexuality of an island of women, the hero first flees back to the womb (the old woman's box), then escapes by aligning himself with a familiar symbol of virility.

How did this happen?

Clearly, in the long run, it must have had something to do with the displacement of the Zafy Ibrahim from their earlier role as the favored caste of internal outsiders, and the adoption of first the pirates, then the Malata, in their place. Left without any notable privileges to defend, the Zafy Ibrahim no longer had any reason to so thoroughly offend the moral standards of their neighbors; once they mixed freely with them, they largely dissolved away as a self-identified group. But there is still the question of why the pirates—who, after all, came from home countries with sexual mores far closer to the Antemoro or earlier Zafy Ibrahim than to other Malagasy (John Plantain was willing to shoot his wife's would-be lover dead on the spot)—were seen as preferable in this regard? The answer, presumably, was that the pirates, once they settled down at least, were not in much position to complain. They might have been in possession of enormous amounts of money and treasure, but they also had an almost complete lack of social or economic capital: no allies to call on, outside of their immediate companions, no real understanding, especially at first, of the customs, standards, or expectations of the society in which they were making their home. They could be rendered entirely dependent on their hosts. As Mervyn Brown[22] pointed out, any pirate who proved too brutal, or even who threatened to abandon his wife for another woman, could be eliminated quite easily by the introduction of poison into the evening meal; in which case, any remaining booty would pass to the hands of his widow and her family.

The result was a classic Stranger King scenario. In many

societies, most perhaps, riches and marvels from faraway lands, even if not borne by mysterious strangers, are considered to partake of the very essence of human vitality.[23] The argument goes like this: every social order understands, on some tacit level at least, that it cannot fully reproduce itself, that certain fundamental matters of birth, growth, death, and creativity will always lie beyond its power. Life is, by definition, something that comes from outside. There is thus a strong tendency to identify those outside powers with both extraordinary, unprecedented people and extraordinary, unprecedented objects, that also appear from the outside. In Malagasy, all this is often quite explicit, since such beings are generally referred to as Zanahary or Andriamanitra, usually translated as "god," yet really a kind of generic term for anything that is powerful, or magnificent, but inexplicable.[24] Obviously there is no guarantee that any particular alien object might be so identified. It could end up classed as so much exotic trash, its bearers as dangerous barbarians. That entirely depends on context, and on the politics of the moment. But if one were looking for the opportunity to replace a class of overbearing ritual specialists by moving directly to the source, this would be the obvious way to do it.

What I am suggesting, then, is that even if Betsimisaraka women and their male kin did not, like the Antemoro, rise up to overthrow the dominant caste of interior outsiders, their embrace of the pirates had pretty much the same effect. The Zafy Ibrahim disappear from the scene. Women are liberated from earlier sexual restrictions—and sexual restrictions, of course, are invariably the means of policing every other aspect of women's behavior as well.

The revolution was effected through mythic means. Marshall Sahlins has documented how, in Fiji, the chief as Stranger King is symbolically married,[25] then "symbolically poisoned"[26] by the daughters of the land. In the Malagasy case this often seems to have happened literally.

WOMEN AS POLITICAL TOKENS

At first glance, the evidence we have would not seem to provide any obvious support for this interpretation.

Here, for instance, is Adam Baldridge's own, rather laconic account of his first stay on Sainte-Marie, from a deposition he later delivered in New York. The ship that brought him there in April 1691 left him behind with a few other men; all but a young apprentice quickly succumbed to fevers. Baldridge and his assistant instantly volunteered to assist his new neighbors in a raid against some of their neighbors on the mainland:

> I continued with the Negroes at Saint Maries and went to war with them . . . In May 91 I returned from the War and brought 70 head of Cattel and some slaves. Then I had a house built and settled on St. Maries, where a great store of Negroes resorted to me from the Island Madagascar and settled the island St. Maries, where I lived quietly with them, helping them to redeem their

Wives and Children that were taken before my coming
to St. Maries by other Negroes to the northward of us
about 60 leagues.[27]

It is not clear who, at first, was fighting whom, but Baldridge
appears to have married not into the Zafy Ibrahim, but into a
clan of refugees from Antongil, the great bay to the north.* A
few years later Henry Watson, who spent some weeks on Sainte-
Marie, testified that there were "two old pirates," Baldridge and
a certain Lawrence Johnston, who supplied passing marauders
with food and ammunition "under pretense of trading to Madagascar for negro slaves":

These two men are both married to country women,
and many of the others are married at Madagascar. They
have a kind of fortification of seven or eight guns upon
St. Mary's. Their design in marrying the country women
is to ingratiate themselves with the inhabitants, with
whom they go into war against other petty kings. If one
Englishman goes with the Prince with whom he lives to
war, he has half the slaves that are taken for his pains.[28]

The phrase "the Prince with whom he lives" seems significant—in many of these early cases, it would seem, pirate
settlers married the daughters of important men and eventually took up residence with them, either in the port of Sainte-

* This would explain why the younger "Adam Baldridge" of 1722 was a ruler in
Antongil, and not Sainte-Marie.

Marie itself, or on the mainland. Especially during the first six or seven years when they were still under pressure to provide the New York and Mauritius slave markets, they clearly did take advantage of those outstanding conflicts—granted, with only mixed success—to obtain captives to sell abroad.

So who were these local "kings" and "princes" constantly referred to in foreign accounts? Robert Cabanes[29] made a careful study of all existing travelers' accounts of the northeast in the two centuries before the rise of the Betsimisaraka Confederation to come up with a plausible reconstruction of how society, in the northeast, actually worked. Then as now, the overwhelming majority of the population of what is now Betsimisaraka territory lived in the various river valleys of the coast, which were considered some of the most fertile on the island. They were divided into perhaps fifty largely in-marrying clans, called *tariky*, each numbering between perhaps six hundred and sixteen hundred people, each with its own territory. The principal crop was rice, mostly grown in shifting forest-fallow *tavy* fields, regularly redistributed, or more intensively in marshes, which tended to be assigned to the *filoha* ("heads") of lineages. In any given village, there was a Great Hall where everyone ate their midday meal together, and collective granaries where each family kept their own stock, but also a collective store any family could draw on in case of shortfall. This is why Flacourt wrote there were no rich and poor among them.

Still, this was by no means an egalitarian society. While everyone had access to the means to sustain life, not everyone had equal access to the means to create it. Just as the heads of villages had multiple wives, so each clan had a dominant lineage, headed by a *filohabe*, or "great head," that managed to keep a large proportion of its daughters to itself (either by marrying them endogamously, or by bringing in husbands for them from other lineages).

Still, these core lineages were somewhat jerry-built assemblages, always on the brink of falling apart. Subordinate lineages tacked on through daughters had a tendency to become disgruntled, split off, and found their own clan.* It wasn't difficult to do so. Land was never in short supply. The chief political problem for a *filohabe* was therefore to prevent this from happening, which required the constant manipulation of the one key resource that *was* in short supply: cattle. The forests of the eastern littoral might have been fertile and thinly populated, but they were not a particularly salubrious environment for raising livestock; still, cattle were absolutely crucial, first of all for resolving disputes (all quarrels were resolved through fines, and all fines consisted of oxen), second for holding communal sacrificial feasts that created ancestors (as they still do),[30] and third for displaying the wealth and power of any given clan to others.

European observers often referred to *filohabe* as "kings" and noted they were frequently at war with one another. On the one hand, the designation is not entirely incomprehensible. They tended to live in magnificent houses, often full of Chinese porcelain and Middle Eastern glassware, surrounded by wives and servants. Yet Cabanes's argument is that the way war was conducted ensured none would ever translate their

---

* This explains the apparent paradox whereby despite the overall patrilineal structure of clans, many have women as their founding ancestors.

position into one of local, let alone regional, dominance.[31] Any clan that accumulated too much cattle would find their village the object of night raids by neighboring *filoha*, aimed at seizing cattle, or captives (usually women or children) who could be exchanged for cattle. Sometimes these escalated into arranged, set-piece battles between the armies of two *filohabe*, which would, after the deaths of one or two combatants, end once again with elaborate negotiations for the exchange of prisoners and redistribution of cattle. All prisoners could not always be redeemed, and thus some would languish, usually in some *filoha*'s residence, as slaves, until their families could summon the resources to recover them. But even this didn't really lead to permanent inequalities, since as Flacourt[32] observed, unredeemed prisoners were ultimately adopted and married into the dominant lineages.

Cabanes[33] argues that war thus became a "means of social reproduction" for the lineage system. The phrase is a bit deceptive since he doesn't really argue that it was *necessary* for clans to make war to obtain the means to marry, reproduce, or create ancestors, but rather, like Pierre Clastres[34] did in Amazonia, that warfare ensured that groups remained small, and their leaders were unable to accumulate genuine coercive power. It does seem true that even the most powerful *filohabe* did not really have the ability to issue orders to those outside of their own households, except in the immediate conduct of warfare. Decisions on matters of communal concern were reached by an elaborate process of consensus-finding at assemblies called *kabary*, whether of villages, clans, or, in the case of matters of even greater import (say, a potential foreign invasion, the sighting of a European ship off the coast), regionally. In Mayeur's words:

> Then there are the great *kabary* of provinces and peoples. The leaders come armed with spear and shield and all military gear. The memory of the title and quality of these leaders, their numbers and the numbers of their followers that curiosity led to these solemn assemblies and motivated to speak, never leaves the minds of the inhabitants. and is made epochal in their traditions. These kinds of *kabary* are held in places capable of receiving a great multitude, usually at the center of the provinces and near the largest villages . . .
>
> Meetings used to be spontaneous. At word of some event a little *kabary* formed and spread the word to everyone's lips. whereon all moved by curiosity came out of their villages, going in quest of and approaching the center of communications, and the *kabary* took place when they found themselves surrounded by all the important people of the land. Provisions were brought because none knew the time they would return.[35]

Deliberations could take days. If the situation warranted, a war chief, capable of leading the forces of a temporary confederation of clans, might be elected to handle the situation. One has to imagine such assemblies were brought together to coordinate trade in cattle and rice with the Portuguese and Dutch vessels that began to appear on the coast in the sixteenth century, and later made the decision to destroy the various military outposts they occasionally tried to set up. Such a great *kabary* must have been convoked to make the decision to launch the coordinated attacks on the pirates in 1697.

In the scholarly literature on Madagascar, Cabanes's essay is considered a landmark of sorts, a model for theoretically informed historical analysis. Deservedly so; still, he clearly overstates the egalitarianism of the society he describes. First of all, he completely ignores the role of the Zafy Ibrahim, and other ritual specialists (as we'll see there were also some Zafiraminia and Antemoro astrologers and magicians in the area as well). If cattle were the "media of communication,"[36] as he puts it, between lineages, then surely it was significant that they could be sacrificed only by members of a specialized caste. Second, there is evidence—Mayeur's text for instance makes it abundantly clear—that the various *filoha, filohabe,* and their warrior entourages did see themselves as constituting a kind of aristocracy. In the Ratsimilaho manuscript they are regularly referred to as *mpanjaka,* "kings," and oral traditions would tend to confirm this, as they almost invariably tell the story of this early period[37] as one of the doings of "kings." And while it is true that clans were not ranked, *mpanjaka* were: thus, for instance, we hear at one point that Ratsimilaho selected as his couriers "young men chosen from the family of Mpanjaka of the first, second, and third class,"[38]* and it is occasionally noted that Ratsimilaho's own mother was the only daughter of a *mpanjaka* of only the second order of nobility.[39] We don't

---

* *Jeunes gens choisis dans la famille des Pandzacas de premier, seconde et troisième classe.*

really know the basis of this system of ranking, but even if these three orders refer only to war chiefs, clan chiefs, and village chiefs, their existence demonstrates that divisions within a clan could translate into something like a graded aristocracy recognized outside the clan itself.

Finally—and this is what's really important for present purposes—rather like Clastres, Cabanes emphasizes how war tended to undermine men's control over other men while simultaneously reinforcing their control over women. Women appear only as tokens of exchange, or wealth to be accumulated. While there seems to have been little effort to control women's sexuality, much of this apparatus acted, directly or indirectly, to control their fertility. Women were kidnapped, redeemed, attached to dominant lineages, but rarely do they appear as actors in their own right.

What's more, the first impulse of these various *mpanjaka* when dealing with the pirates was to extend the women and girls of their lineage as a kind of medium of exchange—presumably, at first, as a way of gaining an advantage over the Zafy Ibrahim. Let us return to Clement Downing's account once more, since he gives us the first written description of the practice. On April 18, Downing's crew anchored off at Sainte-Marie, as part of a mission to identify and eradicate any remaining pirate dens. They found the old fort in ruins, and that the pirates themselves had largely abandoned the island for the mainland. The local "king"—not apparently of the Zafy Ibrahim, since that lineage seems at this time to have been largely driven from the island[40]—greeted them enthusiastically:

On the 19th about Noon, the King and Prince, and the King's two Daughters came on board. The King offered the Captain his two Daughters as a Present, being what they used to offer amongst the Pyrates; for they thought we were all alike: But tho' the Captain refused this kind Offer, the Ladies were accepted by Some of our Officers, who paid dear enough for the Honour; for it cost one of them his Life, and the other was well pepper'd. The King gave the Captain and the Lieutenants an Offer to come on shore, and at their Landing, the King made them Swear by the Sea, that they would be Friends to them, and not Molest them; and for further Confirmation, they compelled every one of them to drink a Glass of Salt Water, mix'd with Gunpowder, in token of Friendship; it being a Ceremony they had learned from the Pyrates.[41]

This text is revealing in any number of ways, but the key point here is that the offer of the daughters of the land, if we may call it that, seems to have originated as part of a ceremony of amity between local *mpanjaka* and visiting pirates, and that it soon became a regular feature in the welcoming of foreign merchants and other visitors. Two things almost all foreign observers remarked on, in such cases, were the elevated birth of the women offered, and their youth.[42] For instance, in 1823, when the French traveler Leguével de Lacombe arrived in the coastal town of Andevoranto, he was greeted the first morning by a coterie of young dancers, putting on a performance in which "they often approached me, without ceasing their movements and gestures that were in no sense ambiguous."[43] Being informed it would be impolite not to choose one as a sexual companion, he pointed to the one he took to be the oldest, one of two daughters of the local *filoha*, who he estimated to be no more than sixteen years of age, and this was greeted with a great cry of joy from her parents.[44] This story, too, ultimately ended with an oath of blood brotherhood between the foreigners and (in this case) one of the girl's family members.

Why, then, young daughters of *mpanjaka*? Presumably because this would assure that, were the resulting alliance to become ongoing, the visitor would be incorporated directly into the *mpanjaka*'s household. An adult woman would have a house of her own, or her husband would be expected to provide her one. Teenagers still lived with their parents. As we've seen, dominant lineages were always trying to attach new members to themselves by marrying them to their daughters uxorilocally. If this did indeed become common practice in dealing with pirates, it would explain Henry Watson's remark about their living with the princes, and how they were so quickly drawn into back-and-forth raiding aimed at the taking and redemption of captives.

)

Still, this was clearly not all that was going on here. After all, if the pirates had simply been incorporated into the existing lineage structure in this way, as hired guns and suppliers of exotic finery, their children would have been absorbed into their patron's lineages and nothing significant would have changed. We'd certainly never have seen the rise of the Malata or the Betsimisaraka kingdom.

So what else was going on?

Contemporary sources provide us with only the patchiest evidence. But there are signs that, while the "kings and princes" seem to have controlled the rice and cattle trade, local markets quickly emerged around the European enclaves, and that these were soon dominated by women. Baldridge's testimony itself suggests this: while he supplied cattle from his own herds to ships that stopped in Sainte-Marie, by 1692, his reports begin to include lines like, "I supplied them with Cattel for their present spending, and the Negroes with fowls, Rice and yams."* He doesn't give any hints as to who these traders were, but many, perhaps most, appear to have been women.† In fact, the sheer numbers of the pirates—at their height there were reportedly at least eight hundred of them, scattered across the northeast—seem to have opened up social possibilities that had never existed before and of which many of the more adventurous young women of the region were quick to take advantage.

---

* Again when Captain Tew arrived in October 1693, they "had some cattle from me, but for their Victualing and Sea Store they bought from the Negroes." Or Captain Week's vessel the *Sussana* in 1695, "I spaired them some cattel, but for the most part they were supplied by the Negroes" (Fox, *Pirates in Their Own Words*).

† Hence for instance Johnson relates how Nathaniel North, having swam naked to shore opposite Sainte-Marie, was mistaken for a spirit except by "one Woman, who had been used to sell Fowls at the white Men's Houses" (*A General History of the Pyrates*, 520). Local markets today tend to be dominated by women.

WOMEN TRADERS AND MAGICAL CHARMS

One day four sisters set out to seek their fortune . . .
                    —beginning of a Betsimisaraka folktale[45]

Contemporary Betsimisaraka oral traditions seem to have almost nothing to say about the pirates. The closest I've come to an account of their arrival from the Malagasy point of view is a text, clearly derived from some local oral tradition, which purports to tell the origins of Ratsimilaho. It's to be found in the Musée Lampy, the local history museum in Fénérive-Est. The names and dates are garbled beyond all recognition,* but the text is important nonetheless:

In that time there was a woman named Vavitiana. Vavitiana was of the Sakalava tribe. Her aim was to look for a husband. She had a friend who was named Matavy. Each day the two girls would go down to the seaside to watch for sailors. These also had, as a second objective, to find the means to engage in trade. These two things preoccupied Vavitiana and Matavy.

In earlier times, life without a husband was difficult; society gave one no consideration; so they sought for the means to attract men. They worked love charms called

---

* In fact, Rahena was Ratsimilaho's mother, Matavy his wife; Vavitiana is the name of a Betsimisaraka prophetess buried in Tamatave from a different historical epoch who had nothing to do with any of this (see Besy, "Les différents appelations de la ville de Tamatave"); by 1774, Ratsimilaho was long since dead.

"ody fitia." Such charms were considered effective. So Vavitiana and her friend were saved.

These two friends did not live in the same place: Vavitiana was here in this region, and Matavy, in the Sakalava region. After a few years, Matavy and her husband had a child who was named Itsimilaho. When he came of age, he was married to another woman, Rahena, and Itsimilaho became Ratsimilaho. In 1774, Ratsimilaho emigrated to Vohimasina as he'd been defeated by king Ralahaiky.

While in European accounts, Malagasy women are sexual "gifts" presented by men to other men, here it's the women who initiate the action. The Malata came about not because foreign pirates established themselves on the coast and took local wives, but rather, because Malagasy women set out to find foreign men to marry; indeed, were willing to use powerful *fanafody*, or medicine, to acquire them. Such medicine, as we shall see, has long been famous in Madagascar, not just for its ability to cause feelings of desire and affection, but also as a means to bend others completely to one's will. Pretty much any magic that is designed to directly control the minds and behavior of others is classified as "love magic."[46]

The account also makes clear the women's motives were not primarily romantic. They were not so much lovelorn as seeking respect (a woman without a husband is given "no consideration"), and the means to engage in commerce. Presumably, then, if they were going down to the beach each day in search of sailors, it was first of all because exotic outsiders, particularly from faraway lands like Europe or Arabia, were automatically seen as having high status (and contemporary sources do often note this was the case), but second of all because sailors—and pirates in particular—were likely to bring with them substantial amounts of tradable commodities. Such women were in search of the means to be not just pawns in some male game, but social actors in their own right.

To this day, Betsimisaraka women are well known for their inclination to form relationships with foreign men, which can then be used as the basis for economic projects. Nowadays this inclination is accompanied by an ethos that men, being whimsical and inconstant creatures, are not really capable of handling money at all; their incomes should really be handed over immediately to their wives lest it be frittered away on senseless indulgences. Jennifer Cole, for instance, describes several men in contemporary Tamatave "who had successful and enduring marriages, [who] told me with pride how they had never once bought their own shirts, as evidence of how completely they trusted their spouses to manage their money."[47] Cole suggests this goes back to colonial-period ideals of proper bourgeois domesticity, and no doubt this is partly true; but there is also a much longer tradition of Betsimisaraka women dominating markets, and forming commercial alliances with wealthy men to act as their commercial agents. Such women were called *vadimbazaha* ("wives of the foreigners"), and they maintained what had by the nineteenth century, at least, become a variety of more or less formalized domestic arrangements with European men, some temporary, some permanent.[48] Most of these *vadimbazaha* were bi- or trilingual (as English gave way to French as the language of trade along the coast), some literate; many, by that time, of mixed descent themselves. Some could boast of a long succession of Vazaha (foreign) husbands and a variety of children from different unions.

In almost every case, these women were also successful merchants in their own right. In fact, as Dominique Bois argues, seaside towns in Betsimisaraka territory at the time could best be described as "cities of women"; they were in the eighteenth century still typically quite small, consisting of a palisaded space containing perhaps twenty to fifty "great houses," the grandest of which were inhabited by *vadimbazaha*, their (frequently absent) husbands, and various kin and servants. In a real sense such women constituted the backbone of such communities, and no decision of importance could be made without them.

In enterprising Malagasy wives, then, pirates found a solution to their basic problem: how to dispose of large amounts of illegally obtained wealth in such a way as to guarantee a secure and comfortable life. They merely had to concede power over its disposition to ambitious women traders. Indeed, for centuries to come, foreign men would remark on the absolute devotion of such *vadimbazaha* to their lovers' economic and politic interests. Some waxed effusive:

> The Malagasy woman, they say, is a sincere friend, who is no less devoted to your interests than to her own. She does not act except with you and for you. And between you and the Malagasy, she is a firm and solid tie which

only death, or your disdain, can break and in which you will find amity, surety, and protection. With such guides one can walk amongst the Betsimisaraka in all assurance.[49]

Only that one phrase, "or your disdain," suggests this is not just a matter of patriarchal submission. The loyalty was expected to be mutual. And in the case of disdain, what might then be expected to happen? Our sources remain vague, but we have a hint in certain nineteenth-century Merina texts, probably dating from the 1870s, that describe forms of magic employed by Betsimisaraka women who became lovers of highland traders. Such women were notorious for taking terrible revenge when their partners betrayed them:

> *Fehitratra*, this is a form of witchcraft carried out by the wives of traders; a man trading will take a lover by the side of the sea, so as to acquire wealth: "you sell things here, and I'll carry goods up and down from the capital." But once he's acquired wealth, he betrays the woman; he doesn't think about her secret powers that might kill him. So he tricks her, and makes off with their common property. But the woman knows how to destroy him with *fehitratra*; she half kills him, she applies a charm to the man that will make him half dead: from the solar plexus on down he's numb; he has no awareness of when he's making water or emptying his bowels, whether it's on the bed or the floor of his house; he's impotent as well. He's been bewitched by his wife by the

sea, but it's only when the merchant returns to the highlands that the disease begins to stir, but then it advances
until it kills him. This is a spell done by the people of the
coast, the Betsimisaraka.[50]*

Such a terrible fate threatens if a man betrays his partner's
trust entirely. If a trader were simply to abandon his partner to
return to his family in the highlands, she might choose a less
humiliating death:

Rao-dia, a charm made by Betsimisaraka bedfellows, the
women kept by those who take to the road to do commerce. The woman roasts a bit of earth that the man has
stepped on, and pronounces the following imprecation:
"if he shall not be mine, he shall not be anyone's! May
he die! And may his wife and children never know what
killed him!" He comes back to town, and the witchcraft
done by his bed-companion follows him on the road, and
when he dies, people say, "but when he arrived he was

---

* Fehitratra, mosavy ny fehitratra natao ny ravehivavy ny mpandranto; ny olona
mandranto manao vady amoron-tsiraka, manao filan-kariana, "mivarotra aty
hianao, ary izaho kosa mitaona entana miakatra sy midina." Ary nony efa mahazo
hariana izy, manao filan-dratsy amy ny vehivavy izy, kanjo tsy fanta'ny ny zavatra
hahafaty azy, fa ny takona no tia' ny. Ary dia mamitaka an-dravehivavy, mifaoka
ny fanana' ny imbonana; ary dia hain-dravehivavy ny famoanan' azy amy ny fehitratra, dia vonoina tapaka ralehilahy asiana mosavy mahafaty tapaka: hatr' eo am-
bavafo noho midina maty ny tapa' ny ambany, dia tsy mahatsiaro tena na handefa
rano na hanao diky, eo am-pandriana sy ny tany itoerana, dia maty fiainana avy
an-kasarotana izy. Famosaviana ny vady an-tsiraka izany; tonga aty ambony ny
mpandranto vao hihetsika ny aretina, ary dia vao mitohy ny aretim-pahafatesana.
Fandramànana atao ny Anindrantany, Betsimisaraka a. As in all cases, my translation is from the Malagasy.

perfectly fine. And then all of a sudden, he just died!"
That's what makes it *rao-dia*.[51*]

These various forms of revenge magic—*fehitratra, manara mody, rao-dia*—still exist (at least in the sense that people still insist they do), and in the community where I worked, at least, were all considered forms of *ody fitia*, or "love magic," along with a whole series of others, such as *fanainga lavitra* (which can cause an absconded lover to go into a trance from which he or she does not awaken until he returns to the caster), or *tsimihoa-bonga* (which confines a lover within a certain perimeter), that were considered *ody fitia*—either because they tended to be used in romantic situations, or because they were ways of bending another to one's will. Love magic was above all about power and control.[52] Now they are no longer seen as typical of any particular geographical region. But the fact that 150 years ago, they were seen as the particular specialty of women from the northeast coast who entered into commercial and sexual alliances with outsiders is surely significant.

If nothing else, all this gives a sense of what, in our initial story, the use of "love charms" to lure and keep foreign sailors might actually imply. There can be little doubt that pirates were informed of such possibilities very quickly; as they settled

---

* *Rao-dia, ny Betsimisaraka ama-mandry, mosavy natao ny ravehivavy azy mpandranto tany an-dalana. Endazin-dravebivavy nilaozana any an' indrantany ny tany no diaviny ny lahy, dia tsitsihina "tsy ahy tsy an' olona iny! Matesa! tsy ho hita ny vadi-aman-janaka ny mahafaty azy!" Ary tonga an-tanana, dia tonga ny mosavy natao ny vehivavy nama-nandry tany an-dalana, ary dia tonga ny mahafaty azy, dia lazainy ny mpilaza, "tonga tsy naninona tsy naninona, dia maty foana tao izy!"; izany kosa no maharaodia azy.*

in with their new Malagasy families, their new friends and relatives would surely have explained all this, insisting (no doubt not entirely insincerely) that they only had their best interests at heart. Given the fact that the pirates were frequently ill, and many died, of malaria and other tropical ailments, one can well imagine the web of rumors that must have quickly surrounded them.

DOMESTIC AFFAIRS

The tendency of many to take multiple wives did not alter any of this, but merely complicated it. Captain Johnson, for instance, at one point writes—in an admittedly rather fanciful passage—about pirates who "married the most beautiful of the Negroe women, not one or two, but as many as they liked, so that every one of them had as great a Seraglio as the Grand Seignior in Constantinople."[53] Others at the time remarked that they became so enamored with the easy life their wives provided that they proved increasingly less inclined to go to sea.[54] A later, nineteenth-century text, this one preserved only in English translation, presenting the scandalized—and clearly, wildly overstated—reaction of a Merina evangelist assigned to a rural Betsimisaraka community, gives a sense of what polygynous life for those with a good deal of stolen wealth might have actually entailed:

When looking for a husband, the woman thinks little about the good character of the man she accepts, but chiefly about how much money and property he has; so good men and working people are not liked as husbands, for these, they say, would want their wives to do work for them; so thieves and robbers even are sought, for these will get property for nothing . . .

Men in good position have four wives up to twelve. But the reason for taking so many is, they say, that they may get work done for them, yet the husband has not the least pleasure or peace, for he is so quarreled over by these many wives of his. The price of cotton cloth there is a dollar for six yards, so when he buys a *lamba* for one of them, all the others think they ought to have the same, although the *rofia* cloth is what they usually wear. The women are never faithful to their husbands, so there is constant trouble. Each one of the different wives has a house for herself, and the husband divides his time among them; and although he may be quite ill and unable to lift up his head, should he fail to give any one her proper share of his attention, she will go off with someone else . . .

They consider it an understood thing that if a man is not at home, the woman is free to go about to others.[55]

This, he explains, leads in turn to endless complex re-arrangements of property, since women who temporarily leave their husbands for another will often require the gift of an ox in order to agree to return (many, he remarks, acquire quite the herd before finally leaving him for good); or, when a man with many wives departs on a trip and one of them moves in with one of her other lovers, it can be arranged for him to come home early, so as to pretend to discover his wife in fla-grante delicto, and demand a hefty fine for adultery (which he and his wife may then split in half).[56]

The pastor is obviously being absurdly sensationalistic. Still, anyone who has spent much time in a Malagasy village knows how much the combination of the prevalence of differ-ent sorts of magical knowledge, and sexual intrigue, can make life almost infinitely complex and provide an unending source of byzantine gossip. If nothing else, life in such communities is never boring.

Particularly unfair is the suggestion that Betsimisaraka women were interested in a prospective husband only for his wealth. This was not even true of foreigners. As Dominique Bois remarks,[57] even penniless Vazaha could find themselves devoted partners; which demonstrates, she notes, that there must have been other values—prestige, hospitality—at play in the embrace of foreigners. To these I would add another: free-dom. Earlier, I remarked that the pirates arrived with much economic capital, but virtually no social or cultural capital. But from the perspective of a potential partner, even the latter has obvious advantages. First, pirates, like other foreigners, didn't arrive with mothers or other family members to interfere with a wife's decisions; second, they came with almost no relevant social knowledge, not even, usually, the ability to speak a lan-guage most people around them understood. This put their female partners in the position not just of intermediaries, but of mentors—if, obviously, in a classically gendered way. In-sofar as those female partners were not (or were no longer) teenagers living in their fathers' homes, this also gave them an opportunity to, effectively, re-create local society—and with the creation of the port towns, the transformation of sexual mores, the eventual successful promotion of their children by the pirates as a new aristocratic class, this is precisely what they were able to do.

Perhaps the single most startling example of this kind of daring innovation comes not from the northeast, but from the southeast, the territory of the old Antemoro and Antanosy kingdoms and the failed French colony of Fort Dauphin. The reader will recall that the latter was finally destroyed when the colonists abandoned (or at least demoted) their Malagasy wives in order to perform a mass wedding with a shipload of women that had arrived from France.

In October 1697, the pirate sloop *John and Rebecca*, fleeing the uprising at Sainte-Marie, was wrecked off Fort Dauphin and a group of survivors took shelter in the ruins of the old French fort. Before long a delegation from the nearby kingdom came to investigate, and one of its members, an elderly princess, announced one of the pirates—the ship's quartermaster, Abraham Samuel, who was the mixed-race child of a Martinique planter and slave mother—was her long-lost son. She had many years before been married to a French colonist, and had borne him a male child, but he had taken the boy back with him when Fort Dauphin was evacuated twenty-three years before. She was convinced that certain birthmarks showed he must be the same boy. Samuel was smart enough to play along, or perhaps at first he didn't completely understand what was happening, but before long, he found himself, through her machinations, named king of the Antanosy. For the next ten years, Samuel ruled under her wing, everywhere accompanied by a bodyguard of twenty pirate companions; among other things he made the kingdom a base of operations for further raids against slaving ships.[58]

The princess's motivations are of course lost to us. But they aren't hard to guess. The Tanosy were ruled by the Zafiraminia, another one of those patriarchal internal outsider groups, among whom women had a decidedly limited autonomy. By adopting a clueless outsider, who could only be entirely dependent on her for his knowledge of local politics, and catapulting him into a position of supreme power, the princess launched a coup that—despite those patriarchal restrictions—put her effectively in charge of the kingdom.

ON THE OPPOSITION BETWEEN MILITARY AND SEXUAL POWER

What I think all this implies is the existence of at least two different domains of human activity in the northeast at the time: on the one hand, a largely masculine sphere dominated by the *mpanjaka* and *filoha*, in which women, much like cattle, were pawns in heroic games, and on the other, a second emergent sphere of magical, commercial, and sexual adventure where women were at the very least equal players, and often had very much the upper hand. The pirates began, inevitably, by being drawn into the first. But over time the women's roles became more and more prominent.

Probably here, too, the insurrection of 1697, when the

pirates came close to being wiped out, marks the crucial break. Captain Johnson's accounts may contain some echoes of what happened, snippets of actual stories mixed in with the author's own speculations and inventions. His account of the fate of Avery's men in his *General History*, for instance, begins, accurately enough:

> The Natives of Madagascar . . . have innumerable little Princes among them, who are continually making War upon one another; their Prisoners are their Slaves . . . When our Pyrates first settled among them, their Alliance was much courted by these Princes, so they sometimes joined one, sometimes another, but wheresoever they sided, they were sure to be victorious; for the Negroes had no Fire-Arms, nor did they understand their Use.[59]*

This, he explained, led to the pirates acquiring the personal harems mentioned earlier. However, before long the pirates' arbitrary cruelties led their Malagasy neighbors to conclude they were more trouble than they were worth.

> Wherefore the Negroes conspired together, to rid themselves of these Destroyers, all in one Night; and as they now lived separate, the Thing might easily have been done, had not a woman, who had been Wife or Concubine to one of them, run nearly twenty Miles in three Hours, to discover the matter to them.[60]

---

* In fact this isn't true; as we'll see, they had guns, just not very good ones.

After this the narrative descends into pure fantasy, but since we know the author did tend to jumble together accounts culled from interviews with retired or imprisoned pirates, tales overheard in seaside or riverside pubs, and his own fictional reconstructions; and since we do know there was such a co-ordinated uprising, and that some Malagasy defended the pirates; this could well be a memory of an actual event.

Whether or not such an event actually occurred, 1697 was clearly a breaking point. After that, careful settler pirates like Nathaniel North, and a host of Malagasy women in pursuit of their own autonomy, began to create something different from the old heroic sphere of battles and contests in which they had first allowed themselves to be drawn. To call this an "emergent sphere" of action, and of value, might seem an overstatement: others would no doubt argue that the pirates were simply being drawn from the political sphere to the domestic one, the domestic sphere in Madagascar often being a rather colorful and adventurous place in its own right. But I think there is evidence, if indirect, that this is indeed the way that many at the time perceived it.

What evidence we have suggests that magic—the domain of *fanafody*, or "medicine"—was particularly contested territory. It is striking, for instance, that Mayeur's Ratsimilaho manuscript, and accounts of warfare in general, never mention charms or incantations, though they do mention other sorts of ritual—since in Madagascar *fanafody* is usually quite central to the practice of war.

Let's return for the moment to our French traveler, Leguével de Lacombe, who we last met being so enthusiastically greeted by the sixteen-year-old daughter of a local chief in the coastal town of Andevoranto. In the course of his travels he invited a well-known ombiasy, or astrologer-curer, to teach him the rudiments of the arts of astrology, divination, and the fashioning of charms.[61]

Malagasy astrology is based on the Arabic lunar calendar and at this time was still very much identified with arcane knowledge from faraway lands; the most famous specialists were the Antemoro and Zafiraminia from the region of Fort Dauphin (the largely Malgachized East African Sunnis and Sumatran Shiite mystics, respectively, both of whom claimed Arabian origins). The former in particular had spread out across the island, using their skills to establish themselves as viziers at royal courts. There appears to have been an Antemoro establishment in Betsimisaraka territory, which manufactured paper out of mulberry bark, mainly, for the writing of spells, and a Zafiraminia settlement near the town of Ivondro.[62] But there were both male and female Betsimisaraka diviners and curers, too.

Lacombe doesn't tell us anything about the origins of his tutor, but he emphasizes that local magical lore seemed to be bound up around two mythological figures, the giant Darafify, and the witch Mahao. Darafify is a familiar character in Malagasy folklore,[63] a kind of paradigm of the benevolent warrior, ruler, and explorer, who crossed up and down the island looking for worthy subjects to rule, creating various features of the landscape, and engaging in occasional battles with rival giants. Mahao, in contrast, is very much a local figure—we know her only from Lacombe. These two existed in clear opposition, one the patron of protective magic, the other, apparently, of love magic and witchcraft. One can get a sense of the terms of the opposition from the stories told about a set of three great lakes that lay in the forests behind the town of Tamatave: Rosoabe, Rasoamasay, and Nosibe.

The first two were twin lakes, and the story is that they were named after two wives of Darafify who used to make their rice fields there (the giant himself kept the strip of land between for his cattle pens). Ferrand records this little story he heard from a Betsimisaraka woman from Tamatave:

> Rasoabe and Rasoamasay were wives of the giant Darafify. They lived on the site of the lakes which the giant had given them to make their rice fields on. Once while their husband was away, they were unfaithful. He learned of it, and on his return cast each into the lake that now bears their name. Each have founded a new village on the bottom of the lake and live there with their cattle and their slaves. It is said that when the water is calm, one can see their houses at the bottom of the lake.[64]

Here, an inappropriately violent response to marital infidelity—this is actually the only instance I'm aware of, in a myth, of Darafify behaving badly—leaves the women suspended in a kind of watery otherworld. A similar, but much more elaborate, story of infidelity and overreaction left Mahao living a similar otherworldly existence at the bottom of the third lake. The stories are clearly inversions of one another;

they form a complementary set. Yet in the second, the implications become more explicit.

Lacombe had reported crossing this lake some time before, and recalled how his guide warned him that men were required to remain absolutely silent while crossing this lake, lest a terrible fate await them.* The passage is worth quoting in full:

> "You should," he added, "perceive in the lake an island larger than the others. There once lived a woman as beautiful as she was wicked: Maháo, daughter of a powerful Antemoro chief named Andriantsay. This prince had taught her the secrets of the art of magic as his ancestors had brought them from Arabia, that she might be useful to men. But Maháo one day surprised her husband asleep on the breast of a young slave; after stabbing him to death, she swore an implacable hatred for all men, and from that time on she made use of her science to harm them.
>
> "Andriantsay, frightened by his daughter's crimes, drove her and her several women accomplices from his realm. They took refuge on the island that we will be circling.
>
> "There the sons of the principal chiefs of the country came one by one to pay tribute to her charms; she pretended to answer their love and brought them inside her palace where she intoxicated them with delights; but

---

* According to Leguével de Lacombe (*Voyage à Madagascar*, vol. 1, 153), this lake was now owned by the Giant of Fire who was Darafify's enemy.

they paid dearly for the favors she accorded them. Having for three days and three nights tasted the sweetness of love, they received from this cruel woman a charm whose effects were soon fatal. Some, seized by dizziness, rushed into the lake, others struck themselves with their own spears.

"In this manner many, many chiefs and valiant warriors perished, including all of the sons of Bémanana— except the youngest, who God had chosen to avenge the deaths of his six brothers. Based on the council of the sage Ratsara, of the line of the Zafiraminia, he traveled to the island, and, the better to conceal his design, abandoned himself to the pleasures in which Maháo engulfed her victims; but seizing the moment when she was fast asleep, he first grasped a giant's tooth that rendered him invulnerable, then pierced her with several blows.

"However a different talisman, that raised Maháo to the level of a spirit, gave her the power to hurt people even after her death.

"She remains, on the bottom of the lake, and hearing the voice of a man is enough to awaken her old hatreds. Let us not talk too much because it would inevitably lead us to the caves wherein she dwells."[65]

It's not clear if the "giant's tooth" is in fact a tooth of Darafify's, but given the parallelism between the two stories one is justified, I think, in seeing an allusion.

The story of Mahao packs together almost every theme that has emerged in this section: the arcane knowledge of internal outsider groups like the Antemoro and Zafiraminia (the Zafy Ibrahim are by this point out of the picture), the sexual rebellion of their womenfolk, the power but also vindictive use of love magic (it is implied that those lured by her charms were lured by her charms in the most literal sense), the opposition of that power to the male warrior class ("sons of the principal chiefs of the country," "chiefs and valiant warriors . . .")—and, in the story at least, the eventual response and victory of the warriors. But theirs is an ambivalent victory. Mahao is dead, but undefeated. She remains under the water, her power unbroken. Even the male warriors whose speeches dominate the great assemblies have to remain silent when they pass over her. And the two principals, Darafify and Mahao, remain locked in permanent suspended opposition within the logic of magical practice itself.

PART III

PIRATE ENLIGHTENMENT

AT THIS POINT WE CAN FINALLY TURN TO THE STORY OF Ratsimilaho, and examine it in its proper context.

As I've remarked, the great political mobilization that created the Betsimisaraka Confederation was not the creation of the sons of the pirates, most of whom were children at the time. But neither was it, in any direct sense, created by the pirates themselves. The pirates were, very definitely, living in the port towns and observing the events in question; they could not but have had an interest in the outcome; but if Mayeur is to be believed, they stayed very much to the sidelines.* The chief actors, aside from Ratsimilaho himself, appear to have been Malagasy *mpanjaka* and sons of *mpanjaka* fighting over access to the port cities that the pirates, and their women allies, had largely created. To some degree the mobilization was simply a reassertion of traditional male values—military prowess, rhetorical prowess in the public assembly, the creation of

---

* Bialuschewski ("Pirates, Slaves, and the Indigenous Population in Madagascar," 423) also cites an otherwise unspecified "oral tradition" that the pirates merely offered support to the Betsimisaraka but did not directly engage in combat on their behalf.

ancestors through sacrificial ritual. To some degree, too, it was a political experiment, fusing together political models and principles derived from the pirates, and from other foreign sources, with the existing political traditions of the coast, to create something with little resemblance to what came before.

In describing this as a proto-Enlightenment political experiment of course I am being intentionally provocative. But I think a provocation is very much in order here. A self-conscious political experiment carried out by Malagasy speakers is exactly the sort of historical phenomenon that, if it did occur, the current historiography would be least able to analyze, or even acknowledge.

Robert Cabanes's essay on the Betsimisaraka Confederation, which saw the confederation as a way of preserving the mode of reproduction of the "lineage system" against the encroachments of the "system of trade," was published in 1977 and might be considered the high-water mark of a certain broadly Marxist strain of analysis.[1] It corresponded to a period when Madagascar, like so many postcolonial societies, was itself experimenting with state socialism. Since then both the larger political situation, and the primary focus and terms of historical analysis, have changed. An age of "globalization" and the emergence of planet-wide bureaucracies fostering the interests of an increasingly narrow economic elite, in the name of the global "market," has also seen the rise of a style of historical writing that focuses above all on international trade, secondly on "local elites" as the prime—or even exclusive—actors in history. While there has certainly been superb historical work on Madagascar that departs from this focus in significant ways,[2] for the most part, those who have written about pirates[3] follow this model. Foreign traders ally with or conflict with local elites. "Elites" are assumed to be in all important ways the same; at best they might divide into "political elites" and "magico-religious specialists," but mainly the assumption seems to be that there must always be elites, that such elites are primarily in the business of accumulating wealth and power, and that if they can be differentiated, it is mainly by how much power and wealth they have so far managed to accumulate. In all this, either popular movements or intellectual currents (other perhaps than "Western" ones)— cosmology, value, meaning—are largely written out of the picture, the first entirely, the second at best to appear as fancy-dress costumes for a series of actors who, no matter how colorful, are nonetheless cursed to obsessive-compulsively enact the exact same play.*

Here is how one contemporary historian summarizes the significance of the wars that gave rise to the Betsimisaraka Confederation:

Despite the fact that the war generated a considerable number of captives, the Betsimisaraka did not manage to profit from the export of slaves until well after the close

---

* Thus, remarkably, almost none of the voluminous literature on the Antemoro caste system sees fit to mention that this caste system was eventually overthrown by a popular revolution in the nineteenth century; likewise the popular uprising against the Zana-Malata that Carayon refers to as the "revolution of Tanibe" (*Histoire de l'Éstablissement Français*, 15–16) is almost never mentioned in histories of the region, or even accounts of the Zana-Malata!

of hostilities. Prior to 1724 the ports of the east coast had been virtually cut off from colonial markets, as there were few if any visits from slave vessels. Encounters with pirates had led to the loss of several trading vessels around the turn of the century, so in the following years slavers avoided this region . . . During the first half of the 18th century most people on the eastern littoral continued to live in largely autonomous villages. The results of archaeological survey show that there were few changes in pottery traditions and little evidence for trade, social differentiation, or a developed settlement hierarchy. Even though these findings reaffirm that the dominant polity was founded by a single charismatic individual rather than through gradual structural changes, Ratsimilaho never assumed the divine and absolute powers of kingship as practiced among the Sakalava. The Betsimisaraka remained essentially a confederation of independent communities, led by powerful *filohany*, rather than a united kingdom.[4]

While Mayeur suggested that Ratsimilaho was careful to make sure as many of the war captives as possible could return to their families, the tacit—actually, not even all that tacit—assumption here is that anyone in a position to send human beings overseas to slavery, misery, and death would certainly do so, at least, if by doing so they were fairly certain they could acquire a better grade of crockery. One has to assume that, given his druthers, the author would himself, like most anyone else, prefer to live in a society whose members were not being sold off as slaves, and where communities were not ruled by one individual wielding absolute power. Language like this—however superficially neutral—is in fact virtually the only way it is possible to look at a situation where a group of human beings, meeting in public assemblies, comes up with a way to fend off slave traders while still maintaining a decentralized and participatory system of self-governance, and *not* see it as a great historical achievement.

I am going to proceed from the position that this was, in fact, a great historical achievement, and that those who put together the Betsimisaraka Confederation—which was not, after all, the brainchild of a single individual—were mature, thoughtful adults with knowledge of a wide variety of political possibilities, not just from Madagascar but Europe and across the Indian Ocean as well. It also seems reasonable to assume they were especially cognizant of the organization of pirate ships and pirate communities since they dealt with both regularly. What I'm going to do in the rest of the section, then, is to (re)read the existing evidence in this light.

It's a little difficult because Mayeur's account does assume that the confederation was the brainchild of a single individual. It's basically a hagiography. Almost every chapter contains several paragraphs devoted to meditations on the exemplary moral and personal qualities of its protagonist; sometimes, contrasting these qualities with that of his antagonist, Ramangano, king of the Tsikoa, sometimes, simply prolonged celebrations of the man himself. Most other characters exist only to advance the plot, or because they died in an interesting way. The full story, then, has to be largely gleaned through asides and implications. But I think this is possible. Mayeur was relying on the memories of Ratsimilaho's one-time companions in arms, recalled when they were in their sixties and seventies. Some elements of the story (combats, maneuvers, oratory, rituals of alliance) are set forth in striking detail; others have clearly been abraded or suppressed. The result is the quintessential heroic narrative; and while the existence of such a genre on the east coast in the eighteenth century is itself highly significant, to understand the full implications of the events described one must go beyond what was considered worth telling one or two generations later, and turn each bit, as it were, sideways, to see it in the context of what's not being said.

INITIAL SITUATION

By 1712, the pirates had largely abandoned Sainte-Marie and were concentrated along the coast: there seem to have been some settled in the great bay of Antongil, some at Tintingue just opposite Sainte-Marie, but the largest concentrations appear to have been in the towns later to be known as Fenerive (Fenoarivo) and Foulpointe.[5]* The latter, it will be recalled, was referred to at the time as Ambonavola; it had been an

---

* "It is to their frequenting of the North and Northeast of Madagascar that are due the Settlements of Tamatave, Foulpointe, Tenerife [Fenerive], and St. Marie, of the Bay of Antongil, of Mananara, and of Baldridge point. One still sees at the bay of Antongil on the island of Marote, in the cove of Navanne, and that of Véringoûtre, iron rings sealed into the rocks along the coast. It was there that they moored their ships when careening" (Mayeur, "Histoire de Ratsimilaho," 191).

entrepôt for provisioning foreign ships with rice and cattle even before the arrival of the pirates, and now hosted Nathaniel North's experimental community, which attempted to apply pirate governance on land.

According to Mayeur, all the ports of the northeast—Fenerive, Foulpointe, Tamatave—had fallen under the control of a military coalition from the south known as the Tsikoa, made up of five clans whose ancestral lands lay in the central third of what was later to be Betsimisaraka territory. Unlike the "People of the North" (Antavaratra) and "People of the South" (Antatsimo), the Tsikoa lived under the sway of "a king, a chief superior to all the particular chiefs of tribes, a despot, absolute master of the goods and lives of his subjects."[6] This king bore the appropriate name Ramangano ("he who does exactly as he pleases"). The Tsikoa's ancestral territory having no ports, Mayeur goes on to explain, they eventually attacked their northern neighbors and easily took control of the whole of the northeast. Mayeur describes the results as simply tyranny for the Northerners:

> Their young daughters were taken away and sold on board the European ships who frequented the coasts, the slightest murmur was punished by slavery and death. The tombs of the ancestors were desecrated. The objects of exchange needed to trade with the Europeans were taken by force and without compensation. Whole villages were deserted, because men, women, children were employed in the transport of goods inland from the edge of the sea. The arrival of a vessel on any point along the northern coast

became the signal for flight of its inhabitants. If they returned it was as much for fear of seeing their crops devastated and villages burned to the ground, than for the duty to ensure any promised benefits.

The Tsikoa established the seat of their dominion over the conquered territory. They made their capital Vohimasina, a village positioned on the mountain of that name, a short distance from Fenerive, rendered extremely strong. It was from there that the Tsikoa tyrant dictated his laws to those numerous tribes who, ignorant of their own strength, sadly bowed their heads under the yoke of the conqueror.[7]

Mayeur's account is confusing. Sometimes he seems to be describing the usual depredations of the slave trade; at others, the emergence of an empire that claimed control over the entire coast.

Now, it seems very unlikely anything like an absolute monarchy emerged out of nowhere in a country that had previously not even known dominant clans. Elsewhere, the Tsikoa are referred to as "a sort of republic,"[8] and Cabanes[9] is probably correct when he suggests Ramangano was, despite his name, really just a particularly effective war chief of a clan coalition of the traditional variety. Mayeur claims the Tsikoa probably emerged in the sixteenth century, and, crucially,[10] at one point gives the game away when he lets slip they were considered responsible for the massacre of European posts established along the east coast in the 1650s. Put all this together and it seems reasonable to conclude the Tsikoa were originally a military alliance formed in defense of the coast, under the initiative of these same five central clans; an alliance that probably at first had no reality except in emergency situations.

The coalition began to change its nature only with the arrival of the pirates, whereon it began to take on a more commercial role. The Abbé Rochon spoke to Tsikoa elders many years after Ratsimilaho's time and got a very different version of the story. The Tsikoa, they insisted, were simply "the most economic and courageous" of the region's people, who had

> left their lands and had flocked in great numbers to the Pirates' places of habitation, with the intention of procuring various trade goods which they felt had utility and convenience. They particularly sought beautiful Indian textiles, Masulipatnam handkerchiefs, muslins, and other more or less precious goods. The inhabitants of the coast, known under the name of Antavaratra and Manivolo, viewed their presence among them with real pleasure; believing they would be failing in their duty of hospitality and affection to the Pirates, had they created the least trouble in the trading of stock and food of all kinds, needed for the provisioning of their ships.[11]

It was not only women traders, then, who flocked to the new port towns from the 1690s onward, but also men; transporting provisions to the ships, for instance, must have required many hands working as porters, drovers, and the like, and these were traditionally male occupations. Presumably, the Tsikoa, who had the disadvantage of distance, fell back on their old military organization to protect their convoys and establishments in the region. Inevitably, that organization got drawn into local conflicts. Even when slave traders were not trying to stir up trouble, the existence of so much concentrated wealth in a society where manly virtue was bound up in a culture of cattle raiding must have led to inevitable unrest—Mayeur elsewhere describes "continual strife, looting of warehouses, burning of villages, abductions of cattle, ruined crops, slavery, misery, and all the scourges of hatred and revenge to which they give birth."[12] Johnson's history of Nathaniel North[13] describes the pirate colony at Ambonavola as always on the brink of being drawn into these conflicts. Finally, when foreign slave traders began to appear in greater numbers again, looking to supply the burgeoning plantation economies of Mauritius and Réunion, it must have made obvious sense to them to ally themselves with a military organization foreign to the region. Before long there was a permanent Tsikoa war chief, and at least two permanent garrisons: a palisaded camp right next to Ambonavola/Foulpointe, and Vohimasina, the Tsikoa "capital," a mountaintop fortress a few leagues inland from Fenerive.

There's no evidence the Tsikoa exacted tribute; they simply took a portion of anything brought in or out of the ports, and carried out raids when slave traders required. This must have meant maintaining some sort of understanding with the pirates who controlled the ports. But as indicated earlier, the pirate settlers had since 1697 become increasingly hostile to the slave trade. The more they became enmeshed in local affairs, the more they would have experienced and judged this kind of arbitrary violence in the same way as

their Malagasy families. Mayeur notes the Tsikoa were careful
to exclude the foreigners' actual children from their exactions,
and give them free passage in and out of the ports, but this was
clearly not enough: all sources agree that when a rebellion did
come, the pirates supported it.

This is where Ratsimilaho comes on the scene.

All sources agree that Ratsimilaho's father was an English
pirate known as Thamo, or "Tom," and that his mother was
named Rahena, the daughter of a chief of the Zafindramisoa
clan. The latter still exists in the environs of Fenerive.[14] Beyond
this, though, they diverge sharply. According to Louis Carayon,[15]
a French officer who lived some years on the coast, his parents
met at Sainte-Marie, but the father died before he was even
born, fleeing an expedition sent against the pirates; his pregnant widow, having inherited his stores of arms and treasure,
pledged all of it to a coalition of chiefs that had arisen to fight
the Tsikoa, on condition that they make her child their king.
The story is remarkable because it suggests the rise of the Betsimisaraka Confederation had nothing to do with Ratsimilaho at
all, but it doesn't work for a variety of reasons.* The standard
account is that of Mayeur,[16] that Tom, Ratsimilaho's father, who
had somehow managed to rehabilitate himself, took the unusual
step of bringing his adolescent son to London to get him an education, along with a few of his Malagasy age-mates, but that
after a few months his son grew homesick and demanded to be

---

* For one thing, it would mean—unless the usual date for the war is wrong,
too—Ratsimilaho was born around 1712, and would have been only eighteen
in 1730, despite his existence being noted by various European sources from
1718 on.

taken back. His father then bestowed on him a great store of guns and treasure, and left him to seek his fortune. This account leaves some open questions, too. How precisely did Ratsimilaho's father manage to go back home, and translate his wealth into sufficient respectability that he could get his children an education?* What sort of education would that have been? Did he remain in England, as Mayeur implies, or continue to play an active role in events? And who were the Malagasy compan-

---

* There has been a good deal of speculation as to the identity of Ratsimilaho's father. Mayeur himself thought he was "Tom Tew," a famous New York–based pirate who took part in Henry Avery's expedition in 1694. This is extremely unlikely, since, unless all existing sources are mistaken, Tew died in the attack on the *Ganj-i-Sawai* and never made it back to Sainte-Marie; anyway, he was not from England but Rhode Island. Hubert Deschamps (*Les pirates à Madagascar*, 199) offers the more plausible guess that Ratsimilaho's father was Thomas White, but if so, there would have to be something very wrong with the received chronology, since Ratsimilaho is assumed to have been born in 1694, and White appeared in Madagascar only in 1704 and is said to have drank himself to death five years later. If I were forced to offer a suggestion, I'd suggest Nathaniel North, who was based in Ambonavola, and who is said to have endeavored to get his Malagasy children a European education—if in Mauritius, not London (Johnson, *A General History of the Pyrates*, 555). Pirates often went by many names and there's no reason North couldn't have been known as "Thamo." But the chronology is still problematic: The real problem, I think, in all these speculations is they assume Ratsimilaho's father must have been a famous captain, perhaps because they can't imagine an ordinary seaman would have been interested in educating his child, or would be in possession of such a large store of booty. But pirate booty was distributed equally, and while crews were more likely to elect literate men as captains, there were no clear class divisions between officers and seamen as there were on other ships. Common sense would also suggest it would be easier for a pirate who was *not* already a famous outlaw to have returned to England without being arrested. It's possible Ratsimilaho's father was one of those who took up an offer from the governor of Mauritius to be pardoned in exchange for a (quite hefty) cash payment in 1716—a number did, and would thus have been free to travel legally (Carter, "Pirates and Settlers," 59–60).

ions? Mayeur claims to have gotten the information from two old men who had accompanied their former king on his trip to London, but there's no information about who they were or what part they played in later events.

I think these are useful questions to ask because all evidence suggests there was something of a creolized, pirate culture, which was not limited to Ratsimilaho or indeed the future Malata. Pirates continued to trade and raid throughout the Indian Ocean in the 1710s and '20s. Ratsimilaho himself, according to one source,[17] had made "numerous voyages," including to Bombay and other places along the Malabar coast; as we've seen, he seems to have served an apprenticeship at the Sakalava court, which at the time was full of pirate advisors;[18] later in life, he used his knowledge of credit instruments to organize his kingdom's trade with foreign merchants.[19] It seems reasonable to conclude this experience was neither unique nor strictly limited to the actual offspring of pirates—and, indeed, even in Mayeur's narrative, no Malata takes any active role in the action; all of Ratsimilaho's closest allies and confederates are young men who, like him, had some exposure to the pirates and to pirate ways, but who are themselves of purely Malagasy descent. Only occasionally do we learn their names, but they crop up periodically in the text: the two anonymous companions who went with him to England;[20] Andriambola, his maternal cousin, and a small band of close friends who accompanied him when he is first forced to flee Ambonavola;[21] Tsiengaly, his "most intimate friend" and second in command toward the end of the war;[22] and so forth.

Some of these companions were Mayeur's informants a half century later, and it would hardly be surprising if in telling the story, they downplayed their own role in events. Malagasy elders are expected to be self-effacing. Their modesty, in turn, would only have reinforced Mayeur's own inclination to center everything on the single figure of Ratsimilaho himself, who could be depicted as an Enlightenment prince and lawgiver who created the Betsimisaraka nation entirely out of his own individual genius. This is not to deny that the creation of the confederation was, in a certain sense, a proto-Enlightenment experiment. It's just one in which the idea that everything came down to a single charismatic founder and absolute monarch was, essentially, a ploy. Much as on pirate ships, it was convenient to develop the reputations of all-powerful and bloodthirsty captains to overawe outsiders, even if, internally, most decisions were made by majority vote; the founders of the confederation found it useful, especially when dealing with outsiders, to maintain the pretext of having an all-powerful king, and the existence of so much stolen finery made it easy to create something that looked like a royal court without having to make any significant reorganization of internal labor regimes.

The confederation, then, was neither the creation of a single man nor the collective creation of the Malata. If the young men who do seem to have taken the leading role in conceiving and creating it took pirate ships, and pirate forms of organization, as one of their models, this, too, would hardly be surprising: these were, after all, the foreign forms of organization with which they were most likely to have direct experience. As Johnson's account makes clear, the pirates had, in fact, self-consciously transferred the organization of their ships onto the land when they elected Nathaniel North "captain" of the pirates of Ambonavola, in a manner that, he insists, was self-consciously designed to impress their Malagasy neighbors as a model of good governance. Even those who had traveled to Europe or India were most likely to have done so in the company of pirates.

Finally, some degree of political synthesis would be exactly what one would expect in a context that historian Kevin McDonald describes as a "hybrid culture, blending the rites and rituals of the Caribbean buccaneers with the customs and culture of the coastal Malagasy peoples"[23]—apparent whether in practices of drying beef, ritual toasting, or contracting pacts of blood brotherhood (pirate *matelotage* and Malagasy *fatidra*). In the next section, then, I'll reexamine Mayeur's manuscript in that light. We have no access, unfortunately, to the deliberations whereby Ratsimilaho's companions conceived their project. But we do know something about the ritual forms by which they brought that project into being, since these were meticulously preserved in popular memory.

THE INITIAL CHALLENGE

Here is how Mayeur's story begins.

In 1712, Ratsimilaho, then eighteen years old and newly returned to Foulpointe (Ambonavola) from his abortive trip to England, decided the only way to rally the Antavaratra against the Tsikoa would be through some kind of dramatic gesture, or "*coup d'éclat.*" He sent his cousin Andriambola to the Tsikoa capital with an oxhorn full of rice, but also wearing a white felana, or badge, on his forehead, a traditional marker of par-

tisanship in war.* Offering the horn to wish prosperity on the
king, he explained that Ratsimilaho had consulted with his
ancestors, who indicated that Ramangano—the Tsikoa war
chief—had no claim to the territory of the north, and that
if Ramangano wished to live in peace with him, he should
return to his own country—though, he added, he was willing
to allow the Tsikoa to retain control of Tamatave, the southernmost port, so that his people would not be completely cut
off from foreign trade. Needless to say Ramangano responded
with contempt. He refused the horn, refused to offer a parallel
gesture, and advised Ratsimilaho to leave Foulpointe immediately, lest he send "the flint and musketball" instead.

Ratsimilaho fled with a few companions, and his stock of
money and weapons, to Sainte-Marie.

It's important to highlight certain aspects of this initial
exchange that have been passed over by previous interpreters.
The account has its hero's father return his son from London
to Ambonavola/Foulpointe but gives no suggestion as to in
what capacity: it merely explains that he tried in vain to interest local Malata or chiefs in a rebellion. But when Ramangano
sends a message through his envoy, he addresses Ratsimilaho
as something more than a mere resident:

> Ratsimilaho will receive neither the Tandroka [horn] nor
> the Vary [rice] from me. I will call up the felana in due time.

---

* Each side, in a conflict, would place a different colored badge on their fore-
heads so as to distinguish friend from foe in combat. In the ensuing conflict,
Ratsimilaho's men wore white felana, and Ramangano's, blue.

Tell him: Ramangano commands the numerous peoples inhabiting the territory from the Manoro up to Angontsy. If he has permitted you to establish yourself at Foulpointe, it was only in consideration of the services that your father has rendered him; but he never denied the obedience you owe him as the country's ruler. He knows that you are the son of a white man of merit, but those qualities do not overcome the fact of his foreignness. Your mother was the daughter of a simple chief of the second class, and you have no right to a share of authority. But since you forget your foreign status and your duties as a subject, Ramangano enjoins you to abandon Foulpointe and to go establish yourself elsewhere. Pray to the souls of your ancestors for inspiration, for you will soon be bearing the punishment due your impudence.[24]

It seems unlikely Ratsimilaho would have required permission simply to continue to live in his father's house. The passage makes sense only if Ratsimilaho is not just a casual resident in the town—a town that, only a few years after Nathaniel North's death,* would have still been full of active and retired pirates, their wives and widows, along with Malagasy kin, traders, and hangers-on—but recognized in some sort of official capacity. His father had been an ally of the Tsikoa, who thus allowed his son, despite his youth, to play some official

---

* If he was, in fact, dead. The date of his murder is uncertain, and it's even possible the unnamed Malagasy enemy who is said to have killed him in his bed was Tsikoa or a Tsikoa ally.

role in the port, presumably, owing to his literacy, language skills, and familiarity with foreigners, as an intermediary or in a supervisory capacity in matters of trade.

This gives the fact that it was Andriambola, Ratsimilaho's cousin, delivering the message a new significance as well. Ratsimilaho presents himself not as a child of pirates, but as "chief of the family of the Zafindramisoa" and speaks in the name of his mother's ancestors; what's more, he is his mother's brother's son, who would otherwise be expected to outrank him, as his envoy—that is, subordinate. So in effect Ratsimilaho was doing several things at once: claiming primacy in his clan, despite the fact that he was of what would normally have been a secondary, "children of girls" lineage; and rejecting the order of authority of the Tsikoa Confederation, both whatever office he held by dint of his Malata status, and the larger ranking system that placed him in second rank.

THE GREAT *KABARY*

To return to the narrative, the small party of rebels soon established themselves on the mainland in the northern village of Ambitsika, at the mouth of the Mananara River at the entrance to the Bay of Antongil, where their defiance won widespread admiration, and *mpanjaka* of surrounding clans came to present them with gifts of cattle, rice, sheep, and poultry. Ultimately, all were invited to a grand *kabary*.

In the context of this book, two things in Mayeur's account of this *kabary* jump out: first of all, the exclusion of women; second of all, the adoption of political ritual that is clearly a synthesis of Malagasy, and pirate, custom.

The exclusion of women demonstrates just how much the creation of the two rival republics, the Tsikoa and Betsimisaraka, was a reassertion of male power against the "cities of women" of the coast. In all the great founding assemblies, women were explicitly banned. What's more, the sources seem to be aware how irregular this is. Here is the relevant passage from Mayeur (note the deleted sentence):

ANNEXE I
EXTRAIT DE MAYEUR NICOLAS, *HISTOIRE DE RATSIMILA-HOE*

The passage is in fact the most explicitly ethnographic in Mayeur's manuscript:

> Malagasy call *kabary* any meeting of a number of individuals for any reason whatsoever, with a specific purpose. There are *kabary* of friends, of families, of villages, of tribes, of entire provinces. ~~Women never take part~~. The importance of a *kabary* rests entirely on its object. Among this curious people, lovers of news and for whom time is nothing, everything is material for *kabary*; a *kabary* might be held to hear the adventures of a traveler, to announce that one has heard cannon fire in the distance, saw a vessel offshore, that new whites have arrived with merchandise; then the comments are endless. There is no matter so trivial that it is not taken up seriously. Reports are usually accompanied by the wonderful embellishments . . . All sit on the ground, legs bent, arms folded over the chest, chins on the knees, a bit of cloth folded over the right shoulder; gravely, they smoke tobacco in a pipe with a terra-cotta bowl and bamboo stem; they pass it after a few puffs; and drink honey wine, or arrack when they have it, in a calabash that is handed round the meeting. These *kabary* are held inside houses, or outside the door when space does not allow.[25]

This is, surely, an image of male sociability, but the exclusion of women is written literally under erasure here: the author, or editor, has crossed it out, since in fact women were not excluded from everyday political discussions, neither in town or village. The Betsimisaraka may or may not have ever had the custom, familiar to the Tanala farther down the east coast, of holding women-only assemblies (*kabarin'ny vehivavy*), to handle matters of women's concern—for instance, to judge crimes against women[26]—but it is extremely unusual for women to be excluded from public discussion entirely. The passage is crossed out because it was self-evidently untrue, at least as a generalization: women took part not only in everyday *kabary*, but in village *kabary*, where matters of public concern were discussed, trials and ordeals conducted. Yet there is no trace of any female presence in any of the great regional assemblies described in Mayeur's manuscript, unless it be among the slaves that are occasionally presented as gifts, ransomed, or liberated. Such assemblies were reassertions of the priority of Darafify against Mahao, of the traditional masculine sphere of war.

OATH-TAKING

Mayeur goes on to describe how the organizers ensured that all were arranged by clan and ranked according to age, rather than "wealth or power," each clan bringing one *mpisaka*, a staff whose bearer was empowered to speak in council. Ratsimilaho began by taking his own clan staff, and addressed the assembly, calling on them to reclaim control of the lands passed to them by their ancestors, whose tombs were currently being desecrated by the Tsikoa.

He finished this long speech by a grandiose enumeration
of the great provisions that his father had left him in the
form of arms and ammunition, priceless objects that in
the minds of these people, are the primary source of all
power and all prosperity.

In the memory of man no more important deliberation
had ever occupied their minds; each saw fit to present his
views; some, terrified by the idea of fighting against an
authority that, while it is true was usurped, was nonetheless strongly established, inclined towards peace;
others were sensible to the misfortunes from which they
wished to see their country freed, but feared the effects
these internal dissensions might have on the prosperity
of their trade with the whites. Others, and they were the
largest number, exalted war, breathed nothing but war,
and promised the happiest results . . . Their opinion carried the day. The war was finally resolved unanimously
and the general command of the Antavaratra [North-
erners] was relegated to Ratsimilaho.

The decision, then, was reached by a prolonged process of
consensus-finding (the organizers had built temporary shacks
knowing deliberations were likely to take several days), and in
the end Ratsimilaho was chosen as *filohabe*, the war chief of a
confederation of the "people of the North." If Mayeur's account
is to be believed, the arguments presented made no appeal to
abstract principles, but only to ancestral right: these were the
lands of their ancestors, desecrated by the foreign presence,
their tombs, literally desecrated by being trodden on, having

the memorial poles, topped with the skulls of sacrificed cattle, pulled down, and the skulls covered with earth.

So far all this seems very traditional—though it should be noted it is common Malagasy practice to invoke ancestral custom when creating something radically new. The real innovation came in the ritual that actually created the new alliance.

Just as the last *mpisaka* had finished speaking, a group of men came out carrying a basket. He placed it in the center of the *kabary*. In a corner of his *simbo* (loincloth) were rolled gun flints, lead balls, gunpowder, a few old grated pieces of broken pot or plate, picked up at the market, a few bits of gold and silver, either in ingot or minted form, and some ginger. He placed a certain number of flints, balls and powder with some other powder that the Antavaratra chiefs had presented, he added a Voule, or bamboo measure of water taken from the nearby river, mixed it all together with the point of a knife, and then motioned to all the chiefs to approach.

Each chief received a small incision at the pit of his stomach; the blood was collected on a piece of ginger, and each took a spoonful of the mixture within the shield declaring "we shall obey you, Child of Tham."

"Return to us the heritage of our fathers, return to us our ports, return to us the trade with the whites." This was repeated as many times as there were chiefs called to take the oath. Then Ratsimilaho took the drink: "I swear," he continued, "to return to you the heritage of your fathers, I will return your ports and trade with the whites, I will return the tombs of your ancestors. Your wives and children will no longer be taken on board the ships of the whites, your husbands will not be sacrificed on the sands of the sea, burned by the fire of the Tsikoa's torches, or pierced by the Tsikoa's spears."

The oath being uttered, the administrator of the oath spoke again in an energetic tone, "may the flints of your enemies be without fire, may their powder be without action, may their bullets never reach you; may pots and pans never be lacking for you to cook your food! May cattle be many in your pastures, rice be abundant in your homes!" Having cut the ginger dipped in blood into as many portions as there were chiefs, he distributed a piece to each, and each swallowed it. "You drank of the brew of well-being," he continued, "now eat of the powerful bread of brotherhood." Each put forth their hand and returned to their place.

Most of these details—the ginger, the mixing of blood, the symbolic tokens—are instantly recognizable to anyone familiar with the literature on Malagasy oath-taking and imprecations. Political oaths typically took the same logic as the ritual of *fatidra*, or blood brotherhood, and to a certain degree as well, ordeals.[27] In each case the contracting parties would invoke a spirit, essentially brought into being through the invocation, conceived as an alien, invisible force of violence whose nature was ultimately unknowable, and call on it to visit terrible punishment on any who violate their newfound commitments. In its more elaborate versions it would involve the death and horrific mutilation of some animal whose corpse was displayed to embody the fate wished on any who failed to do so. One of the earliest accounts we have of such a ceremony in fact is Johnson's description, in *History of the Pyrates*,[28] of an alliance between Nathaniel North, the captain of the pirates at Ambonavola, and an otherwise unknown Malagasy prince—one that must have been contracted only a few years before Ratsimilaho's grand *kabary* and that takes almost exactly this classic form, with the parties locking fingers together and calling terrible disasters to fall on whomsoever would violate their oaths.*

)

The recounting of such alliances seems to have become a genre of oral literature in its own right. While Mayeur notes

---

* "They reciprocally swear to do each other all friendly Offices, to be a Friend or Enemy to the Friend or Enemy of the Party to whom they swear; and if they falsify the Oath they make, they imprecate several Curses on themselves; as may they fall by the Lance, be devoured by the Alligator, or be struck dead by the Hand of God . . ." (Johnson, *A General History of the Pyrates*, 405). I note in passing that later accounts of oath-taking eliminate the bullets, flints, and powder, with one notable exception: the very first account of such an oath from the highlands, in Ellis's *History of Madagascar* (vol. 1, 188–89), where the ceremony is still quite similar to the one described in Mayeur, combining imprecations and wishes for health and prosperity. Descriptions written in the Malagasy language a half century later from the same region (Cousins, *Fomba Gasy*, 91–95; Callet, *Tantara ny Andriana eto Madagascar*, 831–51) have already eliminated the guns, and the blessings, and in this, they resemble the descriptions I heard given spontaneously by informants today.

that the deliberations held at the great *kabary* that created the Betsimisaraka Confederation were the most famous his informants could remember, and in a few places he does reproduce some bits of the back-and-forth argument, by far the greater space is devoted to the details of the oaths—and one has to assume this reflects what the actual informants remembered and felt was worth recounting. The words pronounced, and gestures enacted, were at the same time declarations of independence and constitutional documents, and through them new political realities were quite literally constituted, in the sense of being brought into being.

If this is the case, it is particularly significant that the oath-taking rituals reported by Mayeur—not just this, but also similar ones reported later in the process of creating the Betsimisaraka Confederation—departed in significant ways from the usual model. There are two main differences.

First of all, they are clearly a synthesis of traditional Malagasy oath-taking rituals, and pirate oath-taking rituals. We have already cited the passage in Downing where Malagasy chiefs on Sainte-Marie have their guests drink a glass of gunpowder in seawater, "this being a Ceremony they had learned from the Pyrates."[29] In this ritual, it's not just gunpowder, but also flints and musket balls; but the gunpowder is clearly the most important element, as witnessed by the fact that it is the only one to which each of the chiefs contributes their own share.

Second, the oaths do not take the usual form of calling on some alien spirit to punish anyone who breaks their oaths, and none of the symbolic objects refer to disasters to befall the oath-takers should they do so. This is extremely unusual. In fact, I'm not aware of any other account of a Malagasy *fatidra*, or oath-taking ritual, including any of those I heard about or witnessed in my own fieldwork, in which the invocation of such disasters did not take central part—let alone, in which they were left out entirely. Here, instead, the invocation calls misfortunes only on the allies' enemies—much as in many Malagasy gun charms (*ody basy*),[30] calling on their muskets to fail; and then, as in (say) a sacrifice, wishes health and prosperity on all who take part. None of these elements are normally found in political compacts. This can only be interpreted as a way of saying that the political entity being created is not, in its essence, a form of compulsion, even the voluntary undertaking of responsibilities that become coercive once they are undertaken—a social contract in the classical sense—but the collective transformation of destructive power (the guns and powder) into a force of collective prosperity and well-being.

While most Malagasy political pacts—and many African ones—did take on that classic social contract form,[31] the Betsimisaraka contract as described by Mayeur at least would appear to be a calculated departure, an attempt not to turn violence back on itself to maintain social order, but rather, to turn it into something else entirely.

RATSIMILAHO MADE KING

One should not, perhaps, take this too far, because the next time such oaths were taken, while the new elements (the imprecations against enemies, the invocation of collective prosperity and fertility) were included, a curse was indeed added at the end. Let's skip forward quickly in the story. The newly constituted army descended on and laid siege to the palisaded port town of Fenoarivo. After some initial skirmishes the Tsikoa, who apparently had been using the large marshy fields near the town to grow rice to sell to passing vessels, were lured into a false sense of security, then ambushed while harvesting their fields, allowing Ratsimilaho to invent a mocking name for the Tsikoa: the Betanimena, or "Great Red Mud," for the red soil that clung to their bodies as they fled. (This is the name they have been called ever since.) After a deft feint on Vohimasina allowed the Northerners to storm the town, Ramangano found himself trapped in his mountain capital, having increasing difficulties maintaining his supply lines, and was forced to sue for peace. He offered to cede Fenoarivo and Ambonavola, but asked to maintain control over the southernmost port, Tamatave.

Another great *kabary* was held where Ratsimilaho was able to convince the hesitant *mpanjaka* to accept the deal—by promising that war would begin immediately if any Betsi-misaraka in Tamatave were in any way mistreated. In the resulting treaty, Ratsimilaho was recognized by the Betani-mena as "King of Foulpointe" (*mpanjaka* of Ambonavola), and at the same time, by the Betsimisaraka, as permanent war chief: that is, he would direct operations against the Betani-mena should any new conflict arise.

Before the Northern *mpanjaka* returned to their homes, though, Ratsimilaho and his companions organized a final *ka-bary* at Ambonavola to specify the exact rights and duties that his new office of "chief in perpetuity" would entail. Once again,

Mayeur's text[32] does not specify the political arrangements, but instead lingers at some length over the details of the ritual.

First, one of the assembled *mpanjaka* (he does not say which) declares that Ratsimilaho should become the permanent leader, with the right to pass his position on to his descendants, under the name Ramaromanompo ("he who is served by many") and that all those assembled be henceforth referred to as Betsimi-saraka. This had all clearly been arranged in advance, since

> hardly had the speaker finished speaking than the ad-ministrator of the oath appeared with a shield containing gold, silver, powder, ginger intended to be the seal. All the Mpanjaka approached. He gave them the incision in the pit of the stomach. Having collected the blood on ginger, and poured water in the container, he mixed the drink; then striking the shield, to tell the contracting parties to dip the tip of their spears, he stepped two steps back, and his body straight, eyes raised to heaven, he uttered these words . . . "Good God above all that is good, spirits pro-tective of men, good souls of our ancestors, be witnesses of the covenant this large number of people are making, who pray to you to cast a favorable eye on those who will be faithful to it, and abandon those who violate it."
>
> During this invocation oath those concerned were held by the two hands, foot point pressed against each other and keeping each other a profound silence. When it was finished, the ginger was distributed for them to eat. Then they were presented with the drink contained in the shield of which they each drank three spoonfuls.

The one that offered them started with Ratsimilaho, saying in a loud voice at the moment he put it to his mouth: "Child of Andriamisoa, you drink in the presence of God and your fathers, love for thy people, kindness, protection; You chiefs, you drink obedience and loyalty; may your riches be great if you are faithful. May the powder of your enemies be without force, and their stones without fire; may their bullets never reach you. May your rice fields extend from the seashore to the top of Mount Ambohitsimena, may your flocks cover vast plains, may your children multiply like the leaves of trees. May you finally never run out of water to drink or pans to cook your food." This invocation was repeated as many times as there were parties to whom the oath was administered.

The drink finished, the shield was reversed onto the ground; and in making a few turns on itself, he repeated as many times: "May you be speared; may your bones be sewn into a bag if you do not keep the covenant." After the curse that ended the ceremony all the chiefs linked arms to testify by this common sign of benevolence that they were brothers and wished to be friends forever.[33]

The form of the curse and interlocking of arms is almost identical to the blood brotherhood ritual described in Johnson between Captain North, also of Ambonavola, and his Malagasy allies. The oaths were followed by the immolation of twenty oxen, whereon women entered the camp to lead the celebratory dances, and men, to sing praise for those who had died in the war.

At this point, something very odd happens in Mayeur's text. While he begins the chapter by specifically stating that the assembly had been called to clarify the nature of the new king's powers (chief in perpetuity otherwise being "just a title without its attributions having been explicated"),[34] as soon as he is done describing the ritual, he seems to change his mind: inserting a paragraph, instead, which simply notes that for the Malagasy, power is inherently absolute and limited only by the discretion and character of the king.[35] This seems disingenuous—though whether on the part of Mayeur, or his informants, is hard to say. It seems extraordinarily unlikely Ratsimilaho was really granted such absolute power, even in principle—even Mayeur's text describes him as having taken the same oath as everyone else—though it's in keeping with Mayeur's insistence that the entire Betsimisaraka Confederation was simply an emanation of Ratsimilaho's exemplary personal qualities. It would seem, rather, that the actual negotiation and specification of powers, which must have taken place either formally or informally, is simply left out—or, at best, some of the results pushed to the penultimate chapter,[36] which describes Ratsimilaho's manner of rule: for instance, how he allowed each existing *mpanjaka* to retain his powers, as established by local tradition, but also gave anyone the right to call up *kabary*, attended by the king, at which any unpopular usage or decision might be overturned.

Still, the question remains: Is the contradiction in Mayeur's account a product of the author's personal confusion, or does it reflect a more fundamental tension within the Betsimisaraka polity itself? I think the evidence quite clearly points to the latter. Malagasy sources, too, often insist that monarchs by definition have unlimited power. No doubt Ratsimilaho's old companions insisted, to foreigners like Mayeur, that he did as well. In practice, it was anything but the case.

At this point, the account takes another unexpected turn: Ratsimilaho's final act was to call up several prominent Malata, children of pirates like himself, to shower them with gifts and privately assure them he had no interest in challenging their current situation. In fact, no Malata had attended either of his great *kabary*, or took part in the resulting seven-week war; Mayeur makes frequent mention of the "jealousy" and "scheming" of the other Malata, and Ratsimilaho's worry that they might join the other side.[37]

What the account makes clear is that the privileged status of the Malata already existed; it was created by the Tsikoa Confederation itself, though the Malata at that time did not constitute any sort of coherent group—again, unsurprising, considering that the oldest of them would have been in their early twenties. Why then did the organizers of the new confederation attach so much importance to a group whose economic and military significance could not, then, have been particularly significant?

)

It only makes sense, I think, if we bear in mind the larger context mapped out over the course of this book. As we've seen, the first result of the appearance of the pirates was to allow a large number of ambitious women, most apparently of prominent lineages, hence capable of calling themselves "princesses" in the same sense that local headmen could call themselves *mpanjaka*, or "kings," to essentially take control of their wealth and connections, and, with the pirates, effectively create the port cities that were to dominate the subsequent history of the coast. Part of this project was to break the power of the Zafy Ibrahim who had held the position of intermediaries previously. Ratsimilaho, of course, was himself the son of an ambitious woman of this sort—who, significantly, never once appears in Mayeur's story (though there is no reason to think she wasn't still alive at the time). Obviously, if the pirates' wives had the long-term ambition of turning their children into a new intermediary caste of internal outsiders, to replace the Zafy Ibrahim entirely, these children would be very important—and the key to success would be to ensure that they largely marry one another (or, other foreigners). This is indeed what eventually happened, and one can say that, by granting special privileges to the Malata children, the Tsikoa had already acknowledged this project and even recognized Ratsimilaho himself as part of it (since he seems to have held some sort of position at Ambonavola). Ratsimilaho sidestepped this in challenging the Tsikoa, by identifying himself with his mother's clan, and made common cause with other Betsimisaraka *mpanjaka* to develop the vision of a new confederation; but in negotiating with "the Malata," at this point, it would seem he was really negotiating, indirectly, with the remaining pirates and their wives by assuring them he wouldn't abandon this project of creating a new aristocracy.

The most plausible reading, then, is that the constant

references to the jealousy and behind-the-scenes machinations of the Malata allude not to the Malata themselves, who
were mostly still teenagers at this point, not even to their fathers, who seem to have largely supported the project from
the sidelines, but to their mothers, who had been explicitly
excluded from taking part in the various grand *kabary*.* By
trying to appeal directly to the oldest of their male children,
Ratsimilaho was trying to bypass them, perhaps, but also, indirectly, co-opt them.

  This interpretation is confirmed by subsequent events.

)

After a brief respite, the war did begin again; a clan called the
Fariavahy complained of their treatment at Tamatave; after a
failed attempt at mediation, both sides marshaled enormous
forces, and set about negotiating for allies. A war broke out that
lasted many years. It only ended in 1720, after a prolonged siege
of a Betanimena stronghold called Varangarombato. According
to Mayeur, this war took a completely different form than previous military conflicts in the northeast, since both Ratsimilaho and Ramangano deployed modern techniques borrowed
from Europe: where formerly war had largely consisted of night
raids (*tafikamainty*), the rival confederations used coordinated
daytime maneuvers, the creation of fortified posts, and tech-

---

* I might note in addition that in Malagasy, reference to jealousy, or envy
(*fialonana, ankasomparana*), especially when combined with secret machinations, is almost invariably a euphemism for "witchcraft."

niques of siege warfare. Much of this seems to have been an extension of the militarized forms of trade already common on the coast. In fact, much of the action lies in transporting, blockading, and intercepting shipments of rice, cattle, weapons, and ammunition into besieged towns and military positions, and assembling armies that Mayeur claims—doubtless exaggerating—reached up to ten thousand men for prolonged campaigns. It would have required extremely sophisticated logistics to keep even several thousand adequately provisioned for any significant period of time.

Muskets played a peculiar role in the war. Ratsimilaho's great advantage was his personal possession of two hundred muskets, which he distributed carefully to representatives of each clan at the beginning of the war. What's more, if Abbé Rochon is to be believed, the one way the pirates did intervene in the resulting war was by pretending to supply both sides, but in fact, using the opportunity to exchange overpriced guns for captives and thus recover Betsimisaraka prisoners.[38] Still, it's important to understand what the role of firearms in this conflict really was.

We've already seen how prominent was the role of elements of muskets (flints, gunpowder, bullets) in ritual: just as horns of rice were sent as offers of peace, flints and bullets were delivered to enemies as statements of hostile intent. A combination of both (parts of muskets, and symbols of prosperity) were used in the taking of oaths. As I've already noted, *fanafody* in the usual sense—charms designed to give their bearers miraculous powers—are entirely absent from Mayeur's account, even though they tended to be almost universally deployed in Malagasy warfare, and as we've seen, they are well documented in other contexts. He also makes no mention of the Zafy Ibrahim, Antemoro, Zafiraminia, or any of the other groups that we know to have been active in the region, and to have been specialists in such matters. All of this makes sense, though, if the founders of the Betsimisaraka Confederation were trying to create a masculine, warrior sphere in conscious opposition to the feminine sphere that surrounded the pirates (Darafify versus Mahao again).

I think it's fair to say that guns, in these accounts, substitute for *fanafody*. In a very real sense, muskets *were* magical charms. They were just as mysterious, foreign, arbitrary, and dangerous. It's important to emphasize here that the kind of firearms available in Madagascar at that time were extremely unreliable; European traders tended to unload second-rate stock to non-Europeans; tropical conditions made their use even more unreliable; muskets often either turned out not to fire at all, or to misfire in catastrophic ways. To employ such a weapon in combat was very much a throw of the dice: it might destroy an enemy at a distance with otherwise impossible speed and power; it might also blow up in one's hands. Partly for this reason muskets tended to be borne before military columns in much the way an ody or sampy, a protective charm, might otherwise have been, and often their use was restricted to firing in the air by leaders to announce the beginning of hostilities, or initial volleys before armies closed in for battle with javelins and long spears called sagayes.[39] Ratsimilaho as commander seems to have added some innovations, particularly concentrating fire with his relatively dependable guns on those manning fortifications to provide cover for those storm-ing parapets,[40] a technique he seems to have learned from the pirates.[41] But combat was still largely hand-to-hand.

While most of the strategy of the war concentrated on main-taining or disrupting supply lines—making it, effectively, con-tinuous with trade—actual combat was classically heroic, full of individual exploits, duels, exchanges of personal challenges and insults, much as one would expect to find in a Homeric, Icelandic, or Maori epic. Rather than give an account of the back-and-forth of campaigns and alliances, then, let me provide one description that gives a sense of the temper of the whole.

HEROIC WARFARE

In the early days of the siege of Varangarombato, the most skillful and celebrated warrior on the Betsimisaraka side was a young man of the Fariavahy clan named Andriamahery.

> His skill in the art of handling the sagaye and distance at which he could throw a javelin, the address with which he used European firearms, and even more, his courage and fearlessness, made him a formidable enemy to the Betanimena. There were no assaults, no battles where he did not display a love of glory and the desire to win a bundle of spears to deposit, on his return, at the feet of his beloved. These powerful motives always marked his place in the front row. Anyone who followed him was sure to conquer; anyone who opposed him reaped

defeat or death. This Malagasy Hector had not yet found his Achilles, and Ramangano had stopped counting the Betanimena that his arms had slain.[42]

Andriamahery, he noted, had not yet himself made the oath of allegiance, but his loyalty was such that Ratsimilaho trusted him implicitly. One day, Ratsimilaho ordered him to launch a diversionary assault on some of the mountain posts, as he went off with the main body of troops to intercept a supply column.

The Prince left. Andriamahery obeyed. The action began. The commander of the post, a man of great courage and of advanced age named Mandrirezy saw the fiery Andriamahery at the head of his men, casting aside all that stood in way of passage; Mandrirezy, indignant that a prior wound, from the last battle, might stand in the way of his opposing him. Already four of his men had fallen. Three more were sacrificed on crossing the fence, a fourth fell after crossing.

Mandrirezy could not stand this spectacle. "Mad bull," he said, "your horns shall touch the earth today; they shall be attached to the poles of Betanimena tombs!" He spoke and took a bundle of javelins, and threw them from within the enclosure, then stood leaning on his long sagaye.

Andriamahery saw him. "What are you doing up there, old man?" he said. "Why are you not at home making speeches to your family? That's where you belong. Look: here's something that will make you regret your leaving home." At these words his strong arm launched a javelin; another followed; both hit Mandrirezy's shield. A third pierced his loincloth and embarrassed him. Mandrirezy plucked it out.

"Why?" he said. "Well, here's why." He grabbed the javelin and hurled it back at his enemy. "For you to make speeches to the dead!"[43]

This kind of mutual taunting is characteristic of heroic warfare, where often surrounding action entirely stops when two prominent warriors face off against each other. This is precisely what happened here:

The shaft flew, struck Andriamahery's shield, and tilted toward the earth; then, each reduced to their great sagaye, they advanced on one another and, furious, dealt each other terrible blows. The crashing of their shields could be heard from far away. The sound drew a great press of warriors who ceased shooting, and stopped to watch the battle.[44]

Matters took an unexpected turn, however, when in the midst of a mighty blow Andriamahery tripped and fell onto his rival's spear; Mandrirezy instantly grabbed the body and carried it over the fence back into his own camp. At just about this time, the opposed forces became aware of another duel happening below them: Ratsimilaho, having located the convoy of Betanimena canoes in the woods, had run impetuously into the river, and, after an exchange of blows with Ramangano himself, had to be rescued by his own men, nearly surrounded and fending off a barrage of javelins with a broken buckler.

As soon as Ratsimilaho was rescued, he remembered Andriamahery's diversion and rushed back, only to learn of his demise:

> At these words followed the story of the fatal event, all projects of revenge faltered. Andriamahery no longer has need of help, but Andriamahery's body must enter the tomb of his ancestors. He died bravely. There will come a time that the Betanimena will also weep for him; but now, his body is in the enemy's power, prey to wild animals and laughingstock of his foe. This idea is terrible; it absorbs every other feeling in the hero's soul. He wants nothing but Andriamahery and sends envoys to demand him.
>
> Mandrirezy replies that Andriamahery is his, because he defeated him; he will not deliver him without a ransom.
>
> "What do you require?"
>
> "One hundred oxen and ten slaves."
>
> "You give your luck at too high a price."
>
> "It was not luck that led me to him. I want a hundred oxen and ten slaves, or I'll dismember him and sell the pieces."
>
> "Andriamahery no longer has a father, no brother, only his mother and a sister remain."
>
> "He is still of the Fariavahy clan. Contempt will fall on them if they do not redeem him."

"I am neither father nor brother of Andriamahery. I am not Fariavahy. Yet I will redeem him. I will pay you a hundred oxen and ten slaves tomorrow at sunrise."

"Promise me you will give me a hundred oxen and ten slaves."

"I promise them to you."

"And I will choose the slaves?"

"You may choose them."

"Take Andriamahery. The young man was brave. It was unfortunate."

"So will he be carried to the tomb of his fathers."[45]

There follows a description of the obloquies: Andriamahery's mother and sister,* exhausted since during the battle they had been following the traditional Betsimisaraka practice of dancing to give courage to their menfolk, surrounded by family and slaves, adorned him with "with chains, with earrings, with gold necklaces adorned with coral that Ramaromanompo provided"[46] along with seven mantles—and, two hours before dawn, laid him to temporary rest within a split tree trunk, amid songs of mourning and celebrations of his exploits, having received Mandrirezy's leave to bury him at the very spot where he had died.†

All this shows that women were not, in fact, absent from

---

* What happened to the beloved mentioned earlier is unclear.
† The text notes that at a later date the body would be rewrapped with new cloth and transferred to his ancestral tomb, whereon the usual poles of sacrifice would be erected—the rewrapping an anticipation of later highland *famadihana*.

the scene of combat; just so relegated to the margins the nar-
rator rarely sees the need to mention them. And the fact that
the war endured for years, and that such huge numbers of
people were involved, could only have had an effect on the
balance of power between men and women more generally.

The next morning:

Ramaromanompo gives the order that the hundred
oxen promised shall advance into the space between the
two camps. Fifty slaves walk behind for Mandrirezy to
choose among. Mandrirezy emerges, and leads the hundred oxen back inside the Betanimena palisade, then
chooses his ten slaves from among those of his men who
are prisoners.

"I see that your word is true," he told Ramaromanompo. "So I will one day take the oath with you. So
much wealth for a corpse that the worms will eat!"

"It's for the body of a brave man," replied the prince.
"He is worth the price."

"I take your herds because I have need for them; I take
your slaves because they are my people. But I might sell
the cows and I might trade the slaves. I promise them to
you for this freshly dug earth." And with his finger he
pointed to the grave of Andriamahery.

"Keep the oxen and the slaves, they are the price of
courage."

"I will repay you because I am rich; I will deliver them
to you for Andriamahery's family to sacrifice on his

grave, because I have seen neither the knife of sacrifice nor the feast of the dead."

"Generous enemy, I will one day take the oath with you; I will do so; I will receive your gift and we shall eat together on the stone of memory."

After these words, the two heroes took each other's hands and parted. Each returned to his camp; hostilities were suspended during the night.[47]

Magnificent gestures, sumptuous gifts, all these are, just as much as the boasting and dueling, the very essence of heroic behavior, and Mayeur is quite aware of the Homeric echoes (he at one point even refers to the two as Achilles and Hector)—but the very fact that these details were remembered, fifty years later, makes it clear that the heroic genre did exist in Madagascar, and that the war was remembered as a time when individuals could, through the sheer force of their personal qualities, perform deeds with lasting effects. The events surrounding the death of Andriamahery seem to have been considered particularly important, because they foreshadowed the eventual reconciliation of the two peoples, Betsimisaraka and Betanimena, who would ultimately become one. When Mayeur ends his narrative with the establishment of peace, he duly notes that while by then Mandrirezy was dead, his son, Zahimpoina, fulfilled his father's vow and delivered to Ratsimilaho a hundred cattle and ten slaves to pay for the ransom. Ratsimilaho paid for all the expenses incurred by the transfer and ritual burial of Andriamahery's body, which was made sacred by the immolation of twenty oxen on the memorial stone of the clan tomb.[48]

The story begins and ends with tombs: Ratsimilaho's first speech emphasizes the systematic desecration of the northerners' ancestral tombs by the Tsikoa; the war ends with the transfer of thousands of bodies of war dead into these same tombs, now renewed, a material backbone to the new people that has been created. Much pirate treasure was diverted from the living bodies, and commercial accounts, of the pirates' own wives and daughters to enter the circuits of heroic gift-giving and eventually, to be buried with the heroic dead, so as to become a structure of memory around which the newly created Betsimisaraka were to be organized.

COURT AND KINGDOM, AND THE RISE OF THE ZANA-MALATA

Much treasure, too, obviously, ended up in the new king's court at Ambonavola, gradually to be known as Foulpointe. (The king also maintained an alternative residence in nearby Fenoarivo.) By now it should be apparent that in the east coast during this period—that is, from the time of Henry Avery and John Plantain to that of Count Benyowsky—the ability to maintain the appearance of a powerful court, full of armed guards and bejeweled retainers, tells us very little about the actual power of the "monarch" in question. This is true, at least, if "power" is measured by the ability to organize the ritual labor, and material resources, of the surrounding population.

There is little evidence that Ratsimilaho was able to marshal the population in any sense, other than to raise troops in the event of some outside incursion—much like any other war chief. He did try to improve communications, and create a system of warehouses in each major village, where rice could be stored for export, and travelers could be supported, and to have encouraged the expansion of roads. But such communal granaries already existed; and the transport of bulk supplies to the ports was always a matter that overlapped with military functions. Finally, Mayeur specifies that while some of each local *mpanjaka*'s stockpiles—he estimates roughly a tenth of the whole—were forwarded along to the capital for Ratsimilaho's own warehouses, he also emphasizes that how this was done was left up to the *mpanjaka* themselves, rendering the system largely voluntary.[49]

While Ratsimilaho retained some of the younger members of *mpanjaka* lineages around him as "messengers," and employed his own personal slaves to manage his stockpiles, this seems to have been the extent of any officialdom. Neither was there any permanent council of chiefs, or any indication that Ratsimilaho attempted to create anything like the Merina system of *fanompoana*, where each descent group was ranked according to their particular form of ritual service to the monarchy. Clans remained unranked. Archaeologists, as noted, find no evidence of settlement hierarchies; the system of the three ranks of *mpanjaka* is no longer mentioned. There is no sign the Zafy Ibrahim or any other ritual experts received any systematic recognition or privileges either—their demotion appears to have been permanent.

The one exception to this is of course the Malata, later Zana-Malata, themselves. In the latter stages of the war, Ratsimilaho had been careful to allow those who had by then attained military age to form their own detachments, to put them in command positions where possible, and, crucially, exempted the Malata as a class taking the oaths that bound the other Betsimisaraka—including, of course, himself.[50] The latter is quite remarkable because, since these oaths effectively constituted political society, the Malata thus constituted as standing outside it—as a kind of permanent stranger-nobility.

This became, if anything, more true as time went on. If the creation of the Betsimisaraka Confederation can be considered a kind of masculine riposte to the self-assertion of the women who allied themselves with the pirates, then the rise of the Malata might be seen as a counter-riposte. If we take matters from the perspective not of the king himself, but of the men who arranged to put him on the throne: the problem was that there was nothing to really distinguish Ratsimilaho and any other Malata. His father was just an ordinary seaman, his mother's clan was no more distinguished than any other, the booty he had inherited was impressive, but there's no indication it was uniquely so, and anyway, by the time the wars were over he had given almost all of it away. As other Malata grew older, then, their mothers and maternal kin appear to have done their best to establish them as parallel figures: bold warriors surrounded by guns, slaves, and foreign luxuries, equally capable of engaging with foreign traders and other visitors on familiar terms. This anyway would explain the confusing accounts of visitors like Cossigny in the 1730s, who insisted that Ratsimilaho was just one Malata chief among many—and maybe even, Ratsimilaho's own playful insinuation to Commodore Downing that his father was the most famous pirate of them all.

Their mothers also seem to have done their best to ensure that the Malata exclusively married one another. This was critical of course, since it is what turned the disparate and heterogeneous collection of teenagers that existed at the start of the war into an actual social class: the Zana-Malata ("Children of the Malata"), and eventually Zafi-Malata ("Grandchildren of the Malata"), as they are still called today. The subsequent history of this group[51] is a rich potential field for future research—for some reason no one has carried out systematic ethnographic research among the Zana-Malata or attempted to gather their oral traditions—but according to Alfred Grandidier's *Ethnographie de Madagascar*, which (somewhat scandalously) remains our most detailed source: separate lineages of Zana-Malata gradually came to establish themselves as the dominant lineages within most Betsimisaraka *tariky*, or clans.[52] At the same time, the Zana-Malata as a whole were careful to distinguish themselves from the Betsimisaraka, with different Zana-Malata families marking themselves off by the ostentatious rejection of some aspect of typical Betsimisaraka life: either defying typical gender roles while working in the fields,[53] not carrying out circumcision ceremonies for their male children,[54] or rejecting the custom of temporary burial by placing their dead directly in the family tomb.[55]* In other words, each local group came to have their own local class of stranger-princes, or, as I've termed them, "internal outsiders," who were foreigners to their Malagasy neighbors, but Malagasy to foreigners.

)

The paradox was that this multiplication of little stranger-princes actually seems to have ultimately had the effect of furthering, rather than undercutting, the egalitarianism of the larger society. "Betsimisaraka," originally the name of a political coalition, was adopted as the name for an entire people (and I'm using the term "people" here in that double sense in which it is so often employed in Madagascar as elsewhere: as everyone, but also, as everyone else—that is, the entire population, but at the same time more specifically, those who are not members of the elite). There appears to have been a process of schismogenesis, with descendants of pirates trying to set themselves off from the common people; those who increasingly saw themselves as Betsimisaraka, in turn, defin-

---

* Sylla ("Les Malata") mentions the rejection of circumcision, but characterizes it as typical of all descendants of pirates, and this was taken up by Bloch ("Questions historiques") who suggested that therefore the Zana-Malata were essentially rejecting patriliny and creating kinship only through "matrilineal affiliation through blessing" (see also, Mouzard, "Territoire, trajectoire, réseau," etc.). But in fact Grandidier's original statement is much more modest, since he lists only certain lineages (the Zafy Rabe, Zafimbala, Zafindramisoa, and some others in Antongil and around Fenerive) (Mouzard, "Territoire, trajectoire, réseau"). The list is odd, since the last-listed group is not originally Zana-Malata at all, but was Ratsimilaho's mother's lineage.

ing themselves against the descendants of pirates. Sylla, for instance, reports[56] that many Zana-Malata began to return to the practice of bringing in ritual specialists to slaughter their oxen—the Zafiraminia, in this case, and not the Zafy Ibrahim—and would refuse any meat that had not received such ritual treatment; it was likely in response that the Betsimisaraka, in contrast, developed the unique practice of having each minor lineage choose an elder named the *tangalamena*, a purely local ritual mediator between the living and the dead whose particular bailiwick was the sacrifice of cattle.[57] The same seems to have happened on more subtle levels of everyday comportment: just as travelers' accounts began to stress the haughtiness and arbitrary tyranny of petty Malata princes, they also increasingly came to praise the intrinsic gentleness of the Betsimisaraka, their mild and self-effacing manners.

It is a very common principle, in Madagascar, for egalitarianism to be produced, as it were, as a side effect of imaginary forms of absolute power. The Merina king Andrianampoinimerina used to say that his subjects were equal among themselves because they were all subject to him. Gérard Althabe[58] has written extensively of how this dynamic tended to work itself out in Betsimisaraka villages in the colonial period: for instance, by the evocation of dead kings in tromba ceremonies. Something like that seems to have happened with the Betsimisaraka relation to the Zana-Malata. Everyone was effectively equal in relation to them. Over time, this equality became more and more of a value in its own right.

Finally, the fact that the Zana-Malata's status was based on their wealth and connection with distant lands, and that this made for very little basis for differentiation between them, created a looming dilemma of legitimacy for Ratsimilaho's court. His own personal charisma seemed adequate to hold things together in his lifetime, but he seemed well aware that it would be extremely difficult to pass his position on to his children. His solution was—in the great tradition of what Marshall Sahlins has referred to as "upwards nobility"—to marry back into new sources of mysterious power from distant lands. Ratsimilaho negotiated a spectacular marriage alliance with the Sakalava court of Boina, where he had himself served years before as the King's assistant, so that his son and heir would be able to claim two different kinds of royal ancestry. He forbid his daughter, Betia,* to sleep with other Malagasy, even, apparently, fellow Malata, but eagerly encouraged her to form relationships with European visitors at court. Both projects turned out disastrously. Matavy, the Sakalava princess who became Ratsimilaho's primary wife, quickly made known her disdain for what she presumably felt was essentially a sham court and sham kingdom by exercising a princess's normal rights of sexual freedom to a degree that seems to have been considered generally scandalous. This is said to have undermined the legitimacy of their son and heir, Zanahary, whose real father, it was speculated, might have been almost anyone. Betia ultimately fell madly in love with a French corporal and East India Company agent known as La Bigorne, who took

---

* Betia was queen regnant of Betsimisaraka and the daughter of Ratsimilaho and the Sakalava princess Mamadion of Boina ("Madagascar: Hommage à la Réine Betty à Vacoas," *L'Express Maurice*).

advantage of her blind devotion to undermine the stability of the realm at every point.

In the end, Ratsimilaho was said to have died of debauchery and drink, setting off a flurry of deadly conflicts between his wives and concubines over which was responsible for poisoning him.[59] It seems a squalid end. But his reign, such as it was, was remembered as a golden age. Whatever arrangements his companions and allies made, in creating their decentralized mock kingdom, those arrangements appear to have been successful in maintaining the overall peace and prosperity of the country for thirty years, to have largely insulated the Betsimisaraka from the depredations of the slave trade, all not because they had created something like a modern nation-state (as colonial historians like Deschamps suggested), but precisely because they didn't. If this was a historical experiment, it was, for a time at least, startlingly successful.

CONCLUSIONS

God and Man were inseparable companions. One day God said to Man: why don't you go walk around on earth for a while so we can find some new topics for conversation?
                    —beginning of a Malagasy folktale[1]

I BEGAN BY ARGUING THAT THE WORLD OF THE SEVENTEENTH and eighteenth centuries was marked by a much broader intellectual ferment than we usually imagine. What we call "Enlightenment thought" might have come to its full flowering in cities like Paris, Edinburgh, Königsberg, and Philadelphia, but it was the creation of conversations, arguments, and social experiments that criss-crossed the world. The maritime worlds of the Atlantic, Pacific, and Indian Oceans played a peculiar role in all this, since it was aboard ships, and in port towns, that the liveliest conversations must have taken place. Of course 99 percent of all this has been permanently lost to us. Were the pirates who established themselves in Ranter Bay in 1720 really influenced (as Christopher Hill suggested) by Ranter Abiezer Coppe's "Fiery Flying Roule" of 1649? We have absolutely no way to know. Similarly: Were the Zafy Ibrahim, who greeted the first pirates on Sainte-Marie, really the descendants, as they insisted, of Yemeni Jews? Were coastal conceptions of the divine really influenced by Islamic strains of Gnosticism? We'll never really know that either. But our ignorance is only of the specifics; we do have every reason to believe that people, objects, and ideas from across the Indian Ocean world and beyond were regularly making their way to Madagascar; and that the island had long been just the sort of place where political exiles, religious dissidents, adventurers, and oddballs of every sort were most likely to take refuge—and if Madagascar's subsequent history is anything to go by, did.

After they arrived in Madagascar, these new arrivals spent a very large part of their time having conversations with people who were already living there. One can say this with confidence not just because conversation is always one of the principal forms of human activity everywhere—all humans, throughout history, have divided their time largely between working, playing, resting, and discussing things with one another—but also because in Madagascar, the art of conversation is held in such particularly high esteem. "Among this curious people," Mayeur noted, "lovers of news and for whom time is nothing, everything is material for *kabary*."[2] And there is very much a continuum here from formal assemblies to everyday gatherings of family or friends. In fact, the pleasures of discussion, debate, wit, storytelling, and elegant rhetoric are considered something anyone would, or should, find appealing in their culture. And it often does have that effect, for foreigners who learn the language well enough to understand.

In 1729 a book appeared in London called *Madagascar; or, Robert Drury's Journal, During Fifteen Years' Captivity on That Island*, purporting to be the history of a British cabin boy who, shipwrecked in the south of Madagascar, spent many years there as a slave. Historians have long argued whether it's a forgery. Some even insisted the real author was Daniel Defoe. Eventually, the archaeologist Mike Parker Pearson[3] settled the matter by demonstrating many of the geographical details of the text are so accurate, no one who had not lived in that part of Madagascar could possibly have known about them. For my own part, I read the book not long after returning from Madagascar in 1991 and was immediately convinced of its authenticity when I noticed that the author, when speaking of his Malagasy wife's appeal, made prominent reference to her "agreeable conversation,"[4] and noted his disappointment, on returning to his own people, that European women did not seem nearly so interesting to talk to.[5] This just didn't seem the sort of thing an English author who'd never been to Madagascar would have been likely to have made up. But for me it struck an instant chord of recognition. In Madagascar, sexual allure, and conversational skill, were seen as closely intertwined, and both were considered qualities that made Malagasy culture intrinsically appealing.

All this is important because the origins of Malagasy culture remain something of a mystery. It was once believed that the island was settled by a single population of swidden farmers from Borneo, who spread across it, gradually integrating later waves of immigrants from Africa. Archaeology[6] now reveals a far more complicated picture. Rather than a single homogeneous population spreading out and differentiating, it now seems that Madagascar was first settled by a variety of different groups with next to nothing in common—Malay merchants and their servants, Swahili townsfolk, East African pastoralists, various refugees, and escaped slaves—and that for the first centuries of its habitation, they lived largely independently of one another, and in no sense constituted a single society. At some point, perhaps around the eleventh or twelfth century CE, some kind of synthesis occurred, and most of the patterns and forms now typical of what we consider Malagasy culture appeared, and began to spread across the island. This new cultural grid proved remarkably successful. Within a few centuries, we find a situation not unlike today: a vast island, full of an endless variety of ecosystems, with a population that almost all speak variations of the same language, tell variations of the same stories, carry out variations of roughly the same life-cycle rituals, and otherwise live a thousand local instantiations of a single recognizable cultural grid. We have no idea how this happened. It was certainly not the effect of some conscious political project, or, at least, top-down political project: no rulers at that time had anything approaching the means to unify the island, let alone to impose a uniform culture on its peoples. If anything, it seems to have been founded on a broad rejection of the ethos—the courtly life and monotheistic worship—of urban port towns.[7] To be Malagasy, then as now, appears to have been an explicit rejection of the ways of sea-born foreigners. We don't know how this new cultural grid came to incorporate nearly everyone living on a thousand-mile-long island, but however it happened, sex and conversation must have played a central role.

As so it continues to do. For perhaps a thousand years now, foreign visitors have arrived in Madagascar and have been effectively absorbed. Not all. Some sojourn and leave; others maintain aloof little pockets like the Antalaotra. But the vast majority have become Malagasy and their descendants are now in most ways indistinguishable from anybody else. Again, we don't completely understand the historical dynamics by which this happened. Migrants, for instance, seem to have played a key role in the creation of what are called "ethnic groups" in Madagascar—but not in the way one might think. Since linguistic variation across the island is minor, differences are generally either defined geographically ("sand people," "forest dwellers," "fisherfolk," etc.) or refer to populations that define themselves in opposition to some specific stratum of internal outsiders, such as, say, the Antemoro priest-kings, who insisted they were Muslims even though they had no Korans but only Malagasy-language magical textbooks written in Arabic script, or the dynasties of adventurers that founded the Sakalava kingdoms of Boina and Menabe.[8] Always, these groups were considered alien to those who became a people by defining themselves against them: all those who served the Zafimbolamena dynasty came to think of themselves as Sakalava, even if at any given time they were broken into numerous larger or smaller kingdoms, and even if the rulers were not Sakalava, all those who lived alongside and defined themselves against the Zana-Malata were Betsimisaraka, even if the Zana-Malata were not Betsimisaraka themselves.

THE REAL LIBERTALIA II:
THE BETSIMISARAKA CONFEDERATION

All of this might make Madagascar seem a very unlikely home for Enlightenment political experiments. The fact that so many outsiders were so effectively seduced by and incorporated into this emergent Malagasy culture—a culture whose bearers still pride themselves on its seductiveness—should not lead us to believe that this grid simply annihilated all difference it encountered. Malagasy communities remained, in their own ways, extremely cosmopolitan. We know that people from all over the Indian Ocean, from Java to Oman, traveled to Madagascar, and therefore must have had many long conversations with those they met there, just as Malagasy who traveled must have when they returned. All these conversations have, of course, been almost entirely lost to us. At best we have only the most ambiguous, uncertain traces. Mostly we don't even have that. We can only know they must have taken place.

What I've really been trying to do in this book is to reconsider the history of the pirates in Madagascar, and the rise of the Betsimisaraka, in this light. Pirate ships surrounded themselves with stories of daring and terror—one could even say, armed and armored themselves with such stories—but on board ship, they seem to have conducted their affairs through conversation, deliberation, and debate. Settlements like Sainte-Marie and especially Ambonavola seem to have been self-conscious attempts to reproduce that model on land, with wild stories of pirate kingdoms to overawe potential foreign friends or enemies, matched by the careful development of egalitarian deliberative processes within. But the very process of the pirates' settling down, allying themselves with ambitious Malagasy women, starting families, drew them into an entirely different conversational world. This I argued is the real significance of the stories that Malagasy princesses lured the pirates to land through the use of love magic (*ody fitia*): being drawn into the life of a Malagasy community inevitably means being drawn into a world of endless discussion, speculation, and debate about hidden powers and intentions, and in this new discursive universe, local women clearly had the upper hand. (And of course, as Mervyn Brown pointed out, if any pirate did try to break out of the world of talk and resort to simple violence, it would have been easy enough to simply kill him.)

This, in turn, led many Malagasy men to try to create their own, autonomous circle of conversation: the great *kabary*, from which they attempted to ban women altogether. As I emphasized, we don't really know who these men were, their names and histories. The prime movers seem to have been young, but knowledgeable about the wider world. Some had been to London and Bombay. Many probably spoke at least rudimentary French or English, a few perhaps a smattering of other languages (Arabic, Swahili, etc.) as well. Some might also have been literate. Of one thing we can be certain: most had spent many hours in conversation with active or retired buccaneers, telling stories, speculating on others' motives, exchanging views on money, law, love, war, politics, and organized religion. They also had many opportunities to observe the pirates' ways and practices and compare them to others more familiar. The architecture of the confederation, with its sham autocrat at the center, who could only really give orders during combat, with its pirate oaths and democratic decision-making, emerged above all from those conversations.

Like the pirates' own experiments in settlements like Ambonavola, the Betsimisaraka Confederation was designed, at least in part, to impress outsiders. One need only examine the time line presented earlier. The formation of the confederation corresponded exactly to the moment when pirate kingdoms and pirate utopias were, in fact, being most avidly discussed in France and England. The coalition was first created in 1712, which was also the year that Charles Johnson's play *The Successful Pyrate*, a fantasy about Henry Avery's men creating a kingdom in Madagascar, debuted in London: it is widely considered the first drama to present Hobbes's and Locke's proto-Enlightenment ideas of the origin of kingdoms before a popular audience. The wars ended in 1720, the year Daniel Defoe put out his own book on Avery, and one year before Montesquieu published his *Persian Letters*, considered the first major work of French Enlightenment thought. It was precisely while these wars were going on that pirate envoys—or people pretending to be pirate envoys—were approaching the crowned heads of Europe seeking alliances. Was all this the stuff of conversation across Europe? Clearly it was. It should be borne in mind, too, that the Enlightenment was an intellectual movement uniquely tied to conversational forms; this is true not just of the salons and coffee houses from which its ideas emerged, but even of the prose style it developed—particularly in France— which was witty, light, and conversational, as if propelled by a faith that all intractable social and intellectual problems could melt away in the clear light of intelligent discussion. Were pirate kingdoms and pirate utopias being discussed in the salons of Paris under Louis XV? It's hard to imagine that they weren't, since at the time, they were being discussed virtually everyplace else. How did those discussions inform the (for them) revolutionary conclusions reached by some of those attending those salons about the nature of liberty, authority, sovereignty, and "the people"? We can only guess. What I have tried to do in this book is simply to point out that, until now, we haven't even been asking questions like this. We have constructed a theoretical language that makes it almost impossible to do so. But if, as I once suggested,[9] political action is best defined as action that influences others at least some of whom are not present at the time—that is, that influences others by being talked about, narrated, sung, drawn, written, or otherwise represented—then pirates, women traders, and *mpanjaka* on the northeast coast of Madagascar around the turn of the eighteenth century were global political actors in the fullest sense of the term.

APPENDIX
PIRATE AND ENLIGHTENMENT TIME LINE

EVENTS IN MADAGASCAR

1690—Frederick Philipse sponsors colony on Saint-Marie, Madagascar, under Adam Baldridge (arrived July 17).

1693—Thomas Tew arrives in Madagascar on the *Amity* (October 19).

1694—Henry Avery elected captain after leading a mutiny on the *Charles* (renamed the *Fancy*) and proceeds to Madagascar.

1695—Henry Avery and Thomas Tew's crews capture the *Fateh Muhammed* and *Ganj-i-Sawai*, according to Mughal claims, making off with £600,000 worth of booty. Tew dies in the battle.

1696—Captain William Kidd, sent to suppress piracy, turns pirate and appears at Sainte-Marie looking for recruits aboard the *Adventure Galley*.
—Robert Culliford based in Madagascar, raiding Indian Ocean shipping.
—Remains of the Antanosy kingdom fall under the power of pirate Abraham Samuel.

1697—Insurrection toward end of year destroys fort at Sainte-Marie and attacks several other settlements; Baldridge flees to America.

EVENTS IN EUROPE

1690—John Locke publishes *Two Treatises of Government.*

1696—Henry Avery declared "enemy of the human race" and world's first international manhunt begins.

EVENTS IN MADAGASCAR

1698—Edward Welsh arrives as Baldridge's
successor at Sainte-Marie.
—William Kidd captures the Armenian ship
Quedagh Merchant.

1699—Nathaniel North elected quartermaster
of the *Dolphin*.

1700—Supposed founding of Libertalia
by Captain Misson according to Johnson's
General History of the Pyrates (1724).

1703—Nathaniel North settles Ambonavola,
elected "captain of pirates" in Madagascar.

1704—Thomas White based in Madagascar,
plundering Red Sea shipping.

1705—The *Charles* sails to Madagascar; John
Halsey elected captain.
—Cape Colony report estimates 830 pirates
resident in Madagascar.

1707—Nathaniel North returns briefly to
sea, having been elected quartermaster of the
Charles.
—Thomas White dies in Madagascar of
excessive drinking.

1709—Nathaniel North returns to
Ambonavola.

EVENTS IN EUROPE

1698—East India Act
passed; Britain sends
expedition against
pirates based in
Madagascar.

1701—Public trial and
execution of Captain
William Kidd.

1703—Two English
warships cruise Malagasy
coast looking for pirate
activity but fail to find
any.

1707—Daniel Defoe's
first piece on Henry
Avery appears in *Review*.

1709—*Life and
Adventures of Capt. John
Avery, Now in Possession
of Madagascar* appears in
London, in which Avery
is represented as having
married the Mughal's
daughter.

EVENTS IN MADAGASCAR

1710—Cape Colony report says only 60–70 "miserable and despicable" pirates left in Madagascar.
—Ramangano elected head of the Tsikoa Confederation.

1712—Founding of Betsimisaraka Confederation by Ratsimilaho; first war with Tsikoa.

1715—James Plantain establishes himself at Ranter Bay.
—Dutch merchants meet Ratsimilaho as assistant to Sakalava king Toakafo in Boina.

1716—Ratsimilaho comes to the aid of Mr. de la Bourdonnaye, Governor of Réunion.

EVENTS IN EUROPE

1712—"Pirate envoys" unsuccessfully approach Louis XIV in France.
—Play *The Successful Pyrate* by Charles Johnson about Henry Avery's kingdom of Madagascar debuts in London, disseminating Enlightenment concepts of freedom before popular audiences.

1714—Josef Joumard claims to represent 100,000 pirates to government of the Netherlands, makes unsuccessful bid for support.

1715—Approximate date of creation of Mme Tencin's Enlightenment salon in Paris.
—"Pirate envoys" approach Ottoman and Russian courts.

1718—"Pirate envoys" in negotiations with King of Sweden.

EVENTS IN MADAGASCAR

1719—Pirate Christopher Condent uses Sainte-Marie as base of operations in Indian Ocean.

1720—End of wars to establish Betsimisaraka Confederation; Ratsimilaho establishes "royal court" at Ambonavola/Foulpointe.

1721—Pirate Captain la Bouche on Sainte-Marie, harries shipping lanes to Mascareignes.
—British warships destroy pirate havens at Madagascar, while the French destroy havens in Mauritius and Réunion.

1722—Clement Downing meets James Plantain and his "General" "Mulatto Tom" (Ratsimilaho) at Ranter Bay.
—De la Galaisière affirms Ratsimilaho in power in east coast.

1728—James Plantain flees Madagascar for India.

EVENTS IN EUROPE

1720—Daniel Defoe publishes *The King of Pirates*.

1721—Montesquieu publishes *Persian Letters*.

1724—Captain Charles Johnson (possibly really Daniel Defoe) publishes *A General History of the Pyrates* in London; first work to give detailed accounts of all major pirate captains of the age, and the only source for the story of Libertalia. This becomes the foundation for popularization and idolization of the pirate lifestyle in the following centuries.

EVENTS IN MADAGASCAR

1733—Cossigny meets "King Baldridge" in Antongil Bay; claims there are three local lords on the bay: Baldridge, Tom Tsimilaho, and De La Ray.

1734—Sakalava attacks recorded around Antongil; probable arrival of the Zafindrabay.

1736—French meet King Baldridge's uncle in Antongil; Ratsimilaho sends aid against Sakalava attacks.

1740—French ship captains complain of poor trading and attacks on them in Antongil Bay.

1750—Death of Ratsimilaho.

EVENTS IN EUROPE

1733—Voltaire publishes *Philosophical Letters on the English*.

1740—Hume publishes *A Treatise of Human Nature*.

1748—Montesquieu publishes *The Spirit of the Laws*.

1755—Rousseau publishes *Discourse on Inequality*.

NOTES

PREFACE

1. Graeber, *Lost People*.
2. Graeber, *Lost People*, 353.
3. Markoff, "Where and When Was Democracy Invented?," 673n62.
4. Deschamps, *Les pirates à Madagascar*, 203.
5. Wright, "Early State Dynamics"; cf. Wright and Fanony, "L'évolution des systèmes d'occupation."
6. Carayon, *Histoire de l'Établissement Français*, 15–16.

PIRATES AND MOCK KINGS OF THE MALAGASY NORTHEAST

1. See, e.g., Gosse, *The Pirates' Who's Who*; Baer, "Piracy Examined"; Baer, *Pirates of the British Isles*; Hill, *People and Ideas*; Rediker, *Between the Devil*; Pérotin-Dumon, "The Pirate and the Emperor"; Cordingly, *Under the Black Flag*; Wilson, *Pirate Utopias*; Pennell, "Who Needs Pirate Heroes?"; Rogoziński, *Honor Among Thieves*; Konstam, *The Pirate Ship*; Snelders, *The Devil's Anarchy*; Land, "Flying the Black Flag"; Leeson, *The Invisible Hook*; Kuhn, *Life Under the Jolly Roger*; Hasty, "Metamorphosis Afloat."
2. Downing, *A Compendious History*, 97.
3. Downing, *A Compendious History*, 81.
4. Baer, "'Captain John Avery'"; Baer, *Pirates of the British Isles*, 91–117; López Lázaro, "Labour Disputes."
5. Wanner, "The Madagascar Pirates."
6. Filliot, *La traite des esclaves*; Barendse, "Slaving on the Malagasy Coast"; Barendse, *The Arabian Seas*; Vink, "The World's Oldest Trade"; Bialu-

schewski, "Pirates, Slaves, and the Indigenous Population in Madagascar"; Bialuschewski, "Black People Under the Black Flag."

7. Rochon, *Voyage to Madagascar*, 154.
8. Rochon, *Voyage to Madagascar*, 111.
9. Pearson, "Close Encounters," 401.
10. Brown, *Madagascar Rediscovered*, 96.
11. Linebaugh and Rediker, *The Many-Headed Hydra*, 184.
12. Perkins in Jameson, *Privateering and Piracy in the Colonial Period*; McDonald, *Pirates, Merchants, Settlers, and Slaves*, 89.
13. Nutting, "The Madagascar Connection."
14. Molet-Sauvaget, "La disparition du navire," 493n22.
15. Downing, *A Compendious History*, 114–15.
16. Downing, *A Compendious History*, 129.
17. Downing, *A Compendious History*, 128–29.
18. Downing, *A Compendious History*, 116.
19. Downing, *A Compendious History*, 126.
20. Ratsivalaka, "Elements de biography."
21. Cultru, *Un empereur de Madagascar*, 73; Benyowsky, *Voyages et mémoires*.
22. Ratsivalaka, "Elements de biography," 82.
23. Grandidier, *Histoire de la fondation*; Deschamps, *Les pirates à Madagascar*; Cabanes, "Guerre lignagière et guerre de traite."
24. See, e.g., Deschamps, *Les pirates à Madagascar*.
25. See, e.g., Cabanes, "Guerre lignagière et guerre de traite."

THE ADVENT OF THE PIRATES FROM A MALAGASY POINT OF VIEW

1. Ottino, *Madagascar, les Comores*; Ottino, "Le Moyen-Age"; Ottino, *L'étrangère intime*.
2. Fagerang, *Une famille de dynasties malgaches*; Rajaonarimanana, *Savoirs arabico-malgaches*.
3. Julien, "Pages arabico-madécasses," 1–23, 57–83; Mondain, *L'histoire des tribus*, 5–91.
4. Rombaka, *Fomban-dRazana Antemoro*, 7–8.
5. Ottino, "La mythologie malgache"; Ottino, "Les Andriambahoaka malgaches"; Ottino, "L'ancienne succession"; Ottino, *L'étrangère intime*.
6. Flacourt, *Histoire de la Grande Isle*, 108.
7. Flacourt, *Histoire de la Grande Isle*, 30.
8. Grandidier, *Ethnographie*, vol. 4, bk. 1, 97.

9. Ferrand, "Les migrations musulmanes et juives à Madagascar," 411–15.
10. Ottino, *Madagascar, les Comores*, 35–36; Ottino, "Le Moyen-Age," 214–15.
11. Allibert, "Nouvelle hypothèse."
12. Sibree, *The Great African Island*, 108.
13. See, e.g., Aujas, "Essai sur l'histoire"; Lahady, *Le culte Betsimisaraka*; Rahatoka, "Pensée religieuse"; Mangalaza, *La poule de dieu*; Fanony, *Littérature orale malgache*, vols. 1–2; Nielssen, *Ritual Imagination*.
14. See, e.g., Rochon, *Voyage to Madagascar*, 29.
15. Ottino, "Le Moyen-Age," 214.
16. Dellon, *Nouvelle relation d'un voyage*, 29.
17. Dellon, *Nouvelle relation d'un voyage*, 41.
18. Houtman in Grandidier, *Ethnographie*, vol. 4, bk. 2, 353n35.
19. Flacourt, *Histoire de la Grande Isle*, 137.
20. Ferrand, *Contes populaires Malgache*, 145–7.
21. Grandidier, *Ethnographie*, vol. 4, bk. 1, 10; Grandidier, *Ethnographie*, vol. 4, bk. 2, 137.
22. Brown, *Madagascar Rediscovered*, 98.
23. Sahlins, "The Stranger-King: Or Dumézil"; Sahlins, "On the Culture of Material Value."
24. See, e.g., Graeber, "Radical Alterity Is Just Another Way of Saying 'Reality,'" 1–41.
25. Sahlins, "The Stranger-King: Or Dumézil," 119.
26. Sahlins, "The Stranger-King: Or Dumézil," 109, 125.
27. In Fox, *Pirates in Their Own Words*, 345.
28. In Fox, *Pirates in Their Own Words*, 178.
29. Cabanes, "Guerre lignagière"; compare Esoavelomandroso, *La province maritime orientale*, 41–43, and Mangalaza, *La poule de dieu*, 22–25.
30. See, e.g., Cole, "Sacrifice, Narratives and Experience"; Cole, *Forget Colonialism?*
31. Cabanes, "Guerre lignagière."
32. Flacourt, *Histoire de la Grande Isle*, 23.
33. Cabanes, "Guerre lignagière."
34. Clastres, *Archéologie de la violence*.
35. Mayeur, "Histoire de Ratsimilaho," 200.
36. Cabanes, "Guerre lignagière."
37. See, e.g., Fanony, *Fasina*.
38. Mayeur, "Histoire de Ratsimilaho," 293.

39. Mayeur, "Histoire de Ratsimilaho," 197, 214, 223–24.
40. Gentil de la Galaisière, *Voyage dans les mers*, 537.
41. Downing, *A Compendious History*, 92–93.
42. Bois, "Tamatave, la cité des femmes," 3–5; Rantoandro, "Hommes et réseaux Malata," 109–10.
43. Leguével de Lacombe, *Voyage à Madagascar*, vol. 1, 96.
44. Leguével de Lacombe, *Voyage à Madagascar*, 179–82.
45. Renel, *Contes de Madagascar*, 201.
46. Graeber, "Love Magic and Political Morality"; cf. Fanony, "Le sorcier maléfique."
47. Cole, "The Jaombilo of Tamatave," 895; cf. Cole, "Fresh Contact in Tamatave," and Cole, "Love, Money and Economies."
48. Valette, "Note sur une coutume"; Bois, "Tamatave, la cité des femmes"; Rantoandro, "Hommes et réseaux Malata," 108–12.
49. Rondeau in Rantoandro, "Hommes et réseaux Malata," 110.
50. Callet, *Tantara ny Andriana eto Madagascar*, 106.
51. Callet, *Tantara ny Andriana eto Madagascar*, 107–8.
52. Graeber, "Love Magic and Political Morality."
53. Johnson, *A General History*, 246.
54. Ellis, "Tom and Toakafo," 446.
55. Anonymous, "The Manners and Customs," 71–72.
56. Anonymous, "The Manners and Customs."
57. Bois, "Tamatave, la cité des femmes," 3.
58. Molet-Sauvaget, "Un Européen."
59. Johnson, *A General History*, 58.
60. Johnson, *A General History*, 59.
61. Leguével de Lacombe, *Voyage à Madagascar*, vol. 2, 178–80.
62. Leguével de Lacombe, *Voyage à Madagascar*, vol. 1, 242.
63. Ferrand, *Contes populaires Malgache*; Renel, *Contes de Madagascar*, 49, 186–88; Dandouau, *Contes populaires des Sakalava*, 380–85.
64. Ferrand, *Contes populaires Malgache*, 133–34.
65. Lacombe, *Voyage à Madagascar*, vol. 1, 149–51.

PIRATE ENLIGHTENMENT

1. Cabanes, "Le nord-est de Madagascar."
2. See, e.g., Ratsivalaka, *Madagascar dans le sud-ouest*; Ratsivalaka, *Les malgaches et l'abolition*; McDonald, *Pirates, Merchants, Settlers, and Slaves*.

3. Bialuschewski, "Pirates, Slaves"; Ellis, "Tom and Toakafo"; Randrianja and Ellis, *Madagascar*; Hooper, "Pirates and Kings"; Mouzard, "Territoire, trajectoire, réseau."

4. Bialuschewski, "Pirates, Slaves," 424.

5. Mayeur, "Histoire de Ratsimilaho," 191; Deschamps, *Les pirates à Madagascar*, 197.

6. Mayeur, "Histoire de Ratsimilaho," 194.

7. Mayeur, "Histoire de Ratsimilaho," 195.

8. Gentil de la Galaisière, *Voyage dans les mers*, vol. 1, 527.

9. Cabanes, "Guerre lignagière," 160.

10. Mayeur, "Histoire de Ratsimilaho," 235.

11. Rochon, *Voyage to Madagascar*, 162–63.

12. Mayeur, "Histoire de Ratsimilaho," 213.

13. Johnson, *A General History*, 528, 538–39.

14. Ravelonantoandro, "Les pouvoirs divinatoires des Antedoany de Fénérive-Est," 2.

15. Carayon, *Histoire de l'Établissement Français*, 13–14.

16. Mayeur, "Histoire de Ratsimilaho," 192–93.

17. Gentil de la Galaisière, *Voyage dans les mers*, vol. 2, 526.

18. Ellis, "Tom and Toakafo."

19. Mayeur, "Histoire de Ratsimilaho," 295.

20. Mayeur, "Histoire de Ratsimilaho," 192.

21. Mayeur, "Histoire de Ratsimilaho," 196–98, 209–10.

22. Mayeur, "Histoire de Ratsimilaho," 269–73, 287.

23. McDonald, *Pirates, Merchants, Settlers, and Slaves*, 83.

24. Mayeur, "Histoire de Ratsimilaho," 197.

25. Mayeur, "Histoire de Ratsimilaho," 199.

26. Ravololomanga, *Etre femme*.

27. Graeber, *Lost People*, 63–66, 70, 348; Ellis, *History of Madagascar*, vol. 1, 187–92; Cousins, *Fomba Gasy*, 91–95; Callet, *Tantara ny Andriana eto Madagascar*, 831–51; Decary, *Mœurs et coutumes des Malgaches*, 196–98; Mangalaza, *La poule de dieu*, 26.

28. Johnson, *A General History*, 534.

29. Downing, *A Compendious History*, 93.

30. See, e.g., Vig, *Charmes*, 70–71.

31. Graeber, "Fetishism as Social Creativity."

32. Mayeur, "Histoire de Ratsimilaho," 218–24.

33. Mayeur, "Histoire de Ratsimilaho," 220–21.
34. Mayeur, "Histoire de Ratsimilaho," 218.
35. Mayeur, "Histoire de Ratsimilaho," 221–22.
36. Mayeur, "Histoire de Ratsimilaho," 291–94.
37. Mayeur, "Histoire de Ratsimilaho," 196, 205–6, 223–24, 231, 298, 302.
38. Rochon, *Voyage to Madagascar*, 164–65.
39. Decary, *Coutumes guerrières*; Berg, "The Sacred Musket."
40. Mayeur, "Histoire de Ratsimilaho," 206–19; Berg, "The Sacred Musket," 266–67.
41. Johnson, *A General History*, 531.
42. Mayeur, "Histoire de Ratsimilaho," 250.
43. Mayeur, "Histoire de Ratsimilaho," 250–51.
44. Mayeur, "Histoire de Ratsimilaho," 251.
45. Mayeur, "Histoire de Ratsimilaho," 253.
46. Mayeur, "Histoire de Ratsimilaho."
47. Mayeur, "Histoire de Ratsimilaho," 255.
48. Mayeur, "Histoire de Ratsimilaho," 296.
49. Mayeur, "Histoire de Ratsimilaho," 292; Cabanes, "Guerre lignagière," 172.
50. Mayeur, "Histoire de Ratsimilaho," 231.
51. Sylla, "Les Malata"; Rantoandro, "Hommes et réseaux Malata."
52. Grandidier, *Les habitants de Madagascar*, 201.
53. Grandidier, *Les habitants de Madagascar*, 364–65.
54. Grandidier, *Les habitants de Madagascar*, 403n5.
55. Grandidier, *Les habitants de Madagascar*, 514.
56. Sylla, "Les Malata," 27–28.
57. Rahatoka, "Pensée religieuse"; Mangalaza, *La poule de dieu*; Cole, *Forget Colonialism?*
58. Althabe, *Oppression et liberation*; Althabe, "L'utilisation de dépendances."
59. Gentil de la Galaisière, *Voyage dans les mers*, 528–29.

CONCLUSIONS
1. Dandouau, *Contes populaires des Sakalava*, 366.
2. Mayeur, "Histoire de Ratsimilaho."
3. Pearson, "Reassessing 'Robert Drury's Journal.'"
4. Drury, *Madagascar*, 172.

5. Drury, *Madagascar*, 235.
6. See, e.g., Dewar and Wright, "The Culture History of Madagascar."
7. Graeber, "Culture as Creative Refusal."
8. Graeber, "Madagascar: Ethnic Groups."
9. Graeber, "Madagascar: Ethnic Groups."

BIBLIOGRAPHY

Allibert, Claude. 2007. Annotated edition of Étienne de Flacourt, *Histoire de la Grande Isle Madagascar*. Paris: Karthala.

———. n.d. "Nouvelle hypothèse sur l'origine des Zafi-Ibrahim de l'île Nosy Boraha" (Sainte-Marie, Madagascar). Academia.com, accessed April 21, 2016.

Althabe, Gérard. 1969. *Oppression et libération dans l'imaginaire: Les communautés villageoises de la côte orientale de Madagascar*. Paris: Maspero.

———. 1983. "L'utilisation de dépendances du passé dans la résistance villageoise à la domination étatique." In *Les souverains de Madagascar: L'histoire royale et ses résurgences contemporaines*, edited by Françoise Raison-Jourde, 427–49. Paris: Karthala.

Arnold-Forster, Rear Admiral F. D. 1957. *The Madagascar Pirates*. London: Frederick Muller.

Aujas, L. 1907. "Essai sur l'histoire et les coutumes de Betsimisaraka." *Revue de Madagascar*: 501–15, 543–64.

Baer, Joel. 1971. "Piracy Examined: A Study of Daniel Defoe's *General History of the Pirates* and Its Milieu." PhD diss., Princeton University.

———. 1994. "'Captain John Avery' and the Anatomy of a Mutiny." *Eighteenth-Century Life* 18 (1): 1–26.

———. 2005. *Pirates of the British Isles*. Gloucestershire: Tempus.

Barendse, R. J. 1995. "Slaving on the Malagasy Coast, 1640–1700." In *Cultures of Madagascar: Ebb and Flow of Influences*, edited by Sandra Evers and Marc Spindler, 133–55. Leiden: International Institute for Asian Studies.

———. 2002. *The Arabian Seas: The Indian Ocean World of the Seventeenth Century*. Armonk, NY: M. E. Sharpe.

Benyowsky, Maurice-Auguste Comte de. 1791. *Voyages et mémoires*. Vol. 2. Paris: F. Buisson.

Berg, Gerald. 1985. "The Sacred Musket: Tactics, Technology and Power in Eighteenth-Century Madagascar." *Comparative Studies in Society and History* 27: 261–79.

Berger, Laurent. 2006. "Les raisons de la colère des ancêtres Zafinifotsy (Ankarana, Madagascar): L'Anthropologie au défi de la mondialisation." PhD diss., EHESS.

Besy, Arthur. 1981. "Les différents appelations de la ville de Tamatave." *Omaly sy Anio* 22: 393–94.

Bialuschewski, Arne. 2005. "Pirates, Slaves, and the Indigenous Population in Madagascar, c. 1690–1715." *International Journal of African Historical Studies* 23 (3): 401–25.

———. 2008. "Black People Under the Black Flag: Piracy and the Slave Trade Off the West Coast of Africa, 1718–1723." *Slavery and Abolition* 29 (4): 461–75.

Bloch, Maurice. 1985. "Questions historiques concernant la parenté sur la côte est." *Omaly sy Anio* 21–2: 49–55.

Bois, Dominique. 1997. "Tamatave, la cité des femmes." *Clio: Histoire, Femmes et Société* 6: 61–86.

———. 2001. "Les métis à Tamatave dans la seconde moitié du XIXème siècle." *Annuaire des pays de l'océan Indien* 17: 123–42.

Brown, Margaret L. 2004. "Reclaiming Lost Ancestors and Acknowledging Slave Descent: Insights from Madagascar." *Comparative Studies in Society and History* 46 (3): 616–45.

Brown, Mervyn. 1978. *Madagascar Rediscovered: A History from Early Times to Independence*. London: D. Tunnacliffe.

Cabanes, Robert. 1977. "Le nord-est de Madagascar." In *Essais sur la reproduction des formes sociales dominées*, 87–104. Paris: ORSTOM.

———. 1982. "Guerre lignagière et guerre de traite sur la côte nord-est de Madagascar au XVIIème et XVIIIème siècles." In *Guerres de lignages et guerre d'États en Afrique*, edited by J. Bazin and E. Terray, 145–86. Paris: ORSTOM.

Callet, R. P. 1908. *Tantara ny Andriana eto Madagascar, documents historiques d'après les manuscrits malgaches*. 2 vols. Antananarivo: Académie Malgache. (Reprinted by Antananarivo: Imprimerie Nationale, 1981.)

Carayon, Louis. 1845. *Histoire de l'Établissement Français de Madagascar.* Paris: Gide.

Carter, Marina. 2009. "Pirates and Settlers: Economic Interactions on the Margins of Empire." In *Fringes of Empire*, edited by S. Sameetha Agha and Elizabeth Kolsky, 45–68. New Delhi: Oxford University Press.

Clastres, Pierre. 1977. *Archéologie de la violence: La guerre dans les sociétés primitives.* Paris: L'Aube.

Cole, Jennifer. 1997. "Sacrifice, Narratives and Experience in East Madagascar." *Journal of Religion in Africa/Religion en Afrique* 27 (4): 401–25.

———. 2001. *Forget Colonialism? Sacrifice and the Art of Memory in Madagascar.* Berkeley: University of California Press.

———. 2004. "Fresh Contact in Tamatave, Madagascar: Sex, Money and Intergenerational Transformation." *American Ethnologist* 31 (4): 571–86. humdev.uchicago.edu/sites/humdev.uchicago.edu/files/uploads /Cole/COLE-2004-FreshContact.pdf.

———. 2005. "The Jaombilo of Tamatave, Madagascar." *Journal of Social History* 38 (4): 891–914.

———. 2009. "Love, Money and Economies of Intimacy in Tamatave Madagascar." In *Love in Africa*, edited by Jennifer Cole and Lynn Thomas, 109–34. Chicago: University of Chicago Press.

Cordingly, David. 1995. *Under the Black Flag: The Romance and the Reality of Life Among the Pirates.* London: Harvest.

Cousins, William. 1876 [1963]. *Fomba Gasy.* Edited by H. Randzavola. Antananarivo: Imarivolanitra.

Cultru, Prosper. 1906. *Un empereur de Madagascar au XVIIIe siécle: Benyowsky.* Paris: Challamele.

Dandouau, André. 1922. *Contes populaires des Sakalava et des Tsimihety de la région d'Analalava.* Algiers: Jules Carbonel.

Decary, Raymond. 1951. *Mœurs et coutumes des Malgaches.* Paris: Payot.

———. 1966. *Coutumes guerrières et organisation militaire chez les anciens Malgaches.* 2 vols. Paris: Éditions maritimes et d'outre-mer.

Defoe, Daniel. 1707 [1938]. *A Review of the State of the British Nation: Book 10, June 17, 1707 to November 8, 1707.* New York: Facsimile Text Society, Columbia University Press.

———. 1720 [2002]. *The King of Pirates: Being an Account of the Famous Enterprises of Captain Avery, the Mock King of Madagascar.* London: Hesperus.

Dellon, Charles Gabriel. 1669. *Nouvelle relation d'un voyage fait aux Indes orientales*. Paris: Barban.

Deschamps, Hubert. 1972. *Les pirates à Madagascar aux XVIIe et XVIIIe siècles*. Paris: Éditions Berger-Levrault.

Dewar, Robert, and H. T. Wright. 1993. "The Culture History of Madagascar." *Journal of World Prehistory* 7 (4): 417–66.

Diener, Samuel. 2014. "Free Men and Squalid Kings: Theories of Statehood in A *General History of the Pyrates* and Its Milieu." *UCB Comparative Literature Undergraduate Journal* 5 (1). ucbcluj.org/free-men -and-squalid-kings-theories-of-statehood-in-a-general-history-of-the -pyrates-and-its-milieu.

Downing, Clement. 1737. *A Compendious History of the Indian Wars; with an account of the Rise, Progress, Strength, and Forces of Angria the Pirate*. London: T. Cooper.

Drury, Robert. 1729. *Madagascar; or, Robert Drury's Journal, During Fifteen Years' Captivity on That Island*. London: W. Meadows.

Ellis, Stephen. 2007. "Tom and Toakafo: The Betsimisaraka Kingdom and State Formation in Madagascar, 1715–1750." *The Journal of African History* 48 (3): 439–55.

———. 2009. "The History of Sovereigns in Madagascar: New Light from Old Sources." In *Madagascar revisitée: En voyage avec Françoise Raison-Jourde*, edited by F. V. Rajaonah and D. Nativel, 405–31. Paris: Karthala.

Ellis, Rev. William. 1838. *History of Madagascar*. 2 vols. London: Fisher, Son & Co.

Emoff, Ron. 2002. *Recollecting from the Past: Musical Practice and Spirit Possession on the East Coast of Madagascar*. Middletown, CT: Wesleyan University Press.

Esoavelomandroso, Manassé. 1979. *La province maritime orientale du "Royaume de Madagascar" à la fin du XIXe siècle (1882–1895)*. Antananarivo: FTM.

———. 1981. "La région du Fiherenana à la veille de la conquête française." *Omaly sy Anio* 13–14: 177–86.

———. 1985. "Les 'révoltes de l'Est' (Novembre 1895–Février 1896): Essai d'explication." *Omaly sy Anio* 21–2: 33–48.

Fagerang, Edvin. 1971. *Une famille de dynasties malgaches: Zafindravola, Maroseragna, Zafimbolamena, Andrevola, Zafimanely*. Oslo: Universitetsforlaget.

———. 1981. "Origine des dynasties ayant régné dans le Sud et l'Ouest de Madagascar." *Omaly sy Anio* 13–14: 125–40.

Faller, Lincoln. 2002. "Captain Misson's Failed Utopia, Crusoe's Failed Colony: Race and Identity in New, Not Quite Imaginable Worlds." *The Eighteenth Century* 43 (1): 1–17.

Fanony, Fulgence. 1975. "La riziculture sur brûlis (*tavy*) et les rituels agraires dans la région de Mananara Nord." *Terre malgache* 17: 29–49.

———. 1976. *Fasina: Transformation interne et contemporaine d'une communauté villageoise malgache.* Paris: EPHE.

———. 1985 [1975]. "Le sorcier maléfique *mpamosavy* et l'épreuve de l'ordalie *tangena* en pays Betsimisaraka." *Omaly sy Anio* 21–22: 133–48. Originally in *Cahiers d'histoire juridique et politique* 11: 19–30.

———. 2001a. *Littérature orale malgache,* vol. 1: *L'Oiseau Grand-Tison.* Paris: L'Harmattan.

———. 2001b. *Littérature orale malgache,* vol. 2: *Le Tambour de l'ogre et autres contes des Betsimisaraka du Nord (Madagascar).* Paris: L'Harmattan.

Ferrand, Gabriel. 1893. *Contes populaires Malgache.* Paris: Ernest Leroux.

———. 1905. "Les migrations musulmanes et juives à Madagascar." *Revue de l'histoire des religions* 52: 381–417.

Filliot, J.-M. 1974. *La traite des esclaves vers les Mascareignes au XVIIIe siècle.* Paris: ORSTOM.

Flacourt, Étienne de. [1650] 2007. *Histoire de la Grande Isle de Madagascar,* edited and annotated by Claude Allibert. Paris: Karthala.

Fox, E. T. 2014. *Pirates in Their Own Words: Eye-Witness Accounts of the "Golden Age" of Piracy, 1690–1728.* Fox Historical.

Gentil de la Galaisière, Guillaume-Joseph. 1779. *Voyage dans les mers de l'Inde.* 2 vols. Paris.

Gosse, Philip. 1924. *The Pirates' Who's Who: Giving Particulars of the Lives and Deaths of the Pirates and Buccaneers.* London: Dulau & Co.

Graeber, David. 1995. "Dancing with Corpses Reconsidered: An Interpretation of *Famadihana* (in Arivonimamo, Madagascar)." *American Ethnologist* 22 (2): 258–78.

———. 1996. "Love Magic and Political Morality in Central Madagascar, 1875–1990." *Gender and History* 8 (3): 416–39.

———. 2005. "Fetishism as Social Creativity: Or, Fetishes Are Gods in the Process of Construction." *Anthropological Theory* 5 (4): 405–36.

———. 2007a. *Lost People: Magic and the Legacy of Slavery in Madagascar.* Bloomington: Indiana University Press.

———. 2007b. "Madagascar: Ethnic Groups." In *The New Encyclopedia of Africa*, vol. 3, edited by John Middleton and Joseph C. Miller, 430–35. Detroit: Gale Cengage Learning.

———. 2013. "Culture as Creative Refusal." *Cambridge Anthropology* 31 (2): 1–19.

———. 2015. "Radical Alterity Is Just Another Way of Saying 'Reality': A Response to Eduardo Viveiros de Castro." *HAU* 5 (2): 1–41.

Grandidier, Alfred. 1908. *Ethnographie*. Vol. 4, book 1, of *Histoire physique, naturelle et politique de Madagascar*. Paris: Imprimerie Nationale.

———. 1914. *Ethnographie*. Vol. 4, book 2, of *Histoire physique, naturelle et politique de Madagascar*. Paris: Imprimerie Nationale.

———. 1917. *Les habitants de Madagascar, la famille malgache (fin), rapports sociaux des Malgaches, vie matérielle à Madagascar, les croyances et la vie religieuse à Madagascar*. Vol. 4, book 3, of *Histoire physique, naturelle et politique de Madagascar*. Paris: Imprimerie Nationale.

Grandidier, Alfred, and Guillaume Grandidier. 1907. *Collection des ouvrages anciens concernant Madagascar*. Vol. 5 of *Ouvrages ou extraits d'ouvrages anglais, hollandais, portugais, espagnols, suédois et russes, 1718–1800*. Paris: Union Coloniale, Comité de Madagascar.

Grandidier, Guillaume. 1898. *Histoire de la fondation du royaume Betsimisaraka*. Paris: Augustine Challamel.

Haring, Lee. 1982. *Malagasy tale index*. Helsinski: Academia Scientiarum Fennica.

Hasty, William. 2014. "Metamorphosis Afloat: Pirate Ships, Politics and Process, c.1680–1730." *Mobilities* 9 (3): 350–68.

Hill, Christopher. 1986. *People and Ideas in Seventeenth-Century England*. Vol. 3 of *Collected Essays*. Brighton: Harvester Press.

Hooper, Jane. 2011. "Pirates and Kings: Power on the Shores of Early Modern Madagascar and the Indian Ocean." *Journal of World History* 20 (2): 215–42.

Jameson, J. Franklin, ed. 1970. *Privateering and Piracy in the Colonial Period: Illustrative Documents*. New York: Augustus M. Kelley.

Johnson, Captain Charles. 1724 [1972]. *A General History of the Pyrates*. London: Dent.

Julien, Gustave. 1929. "Pages arabico-madécasses." In *Annales de l'Académie des sciences coloniales*, vol. 3, 1–123. Paris: Société d'Éditions Géographiques, Maritimes et Coloniales.

Kay, Carol. 1988. *Political Constructions: Defoe, Richardson, and Sterne in*

Relation to Hobbes, Hume, and Burke. Ithaca, NY: Cornell University Press.

Konstam, Angus. 2003. *The Pirate Ship, 1660–1730.* Oxford: Osprey.

Kuhn, Gabriel. 2010. *Life Under the Jolly Roger: Reflections on Golden Age Piracy.* Oakland, CA: PM Press.

Lahady, Pascal. 1979. *Le culte Betsimisaraka et son système symbolique.* Fianarantsoa: Librairie Ambozontany.

Land, Chris. 2007. "Flying the Black Flag: Revolt, Revolution, and the Social Organization of Piracy in the 'Golden Age.'" *Management and Organization Theory* 2 (2): 169–92.

Leeson, P. T. 2009. *The Invisible Hook: The Hidden Economics of Pirates.* Princeton, NJ: Princeton University Press.

Leguével de Lacombe, B. F. 1840. *Voyage à Madagascar et aux Îles Comores (1823 à 1830).* 2 vols. Paris: Louis Dessart.

Linebaugh, Peter, and Marcus Rediker. 2000. *The Many-Headed Hydra: Sailors, Slaves, Commoners, and the Hidden History of the Revolutionary Atlantic.* Boston: Beacon Press.

Lombard, Jacques. 1976. "Zatovo qui n'a pas été créé par Dieu: Un conte sakalava traduit et commenté." *Asie du Sud Est et Monde Insulindien* 7: 165–223.

López Lázaro, Fabio. 2010. "Labour Disputes, Ethnic Quarrels and Early Modern Piracy: A Mixed Hispano-Anglo-Dutch Squadron and the Causes of Captain Every's 1694 Mutiny." *International Journal of Maritime History* 22 (2): 73–111.

"Madagascar: Hommage à la Réine Betty à Vacoas." *L'Express Maurice,* October 17, 2010. https://www.lexpress.mu/article/madagascar-hommage-%C3%A0-la-r%C3%A9ine-betty-%C3%A0-vacoas.

Mangalaza, Eugène Régis. 1994. *La poule de dieu: Essai d'anthropologie philosophique chez les Betsimisaraka (Madagascar).* Bordeaux: PUB.

"The Manners and Customs, Superstitions, and Dialect of the Betsimisaraka." 1897. *Antananarivo Annual and Madagascar Magazine* 21: 67–75.

Markoff, John. 1999. "Where and When Was Democracy Invented?" *Comparative Studies in Society and History* 41 (4): 660–90.

Mayeur, Nicolas. 1806. "Histoire de Ratsimilaho (1695–1750), roi de Foulpointe et des Betsimisaraka, rédigé par Barthélémy Huet de Froberville, 1806." British Museum, ADD-MSS 18129.

McDonald, Kevin P. 2015. *Pirates, Merchants, Settlers, and Slaves: Colonial*

America and the Indo-Atlantic World. Berkeley: University of California Press.

Molet-Sauvaget, Anne. 1997. "Un Européen, roi 'legitime' de Fort-Dauphin au XVIIIe siècle: Le pirate Abraham Samuel." *Etudes Ocean Indien* 23–4: 211–21.

———. 2000. "La disparition du navire 'Ridderschap van Holland' à Madagascar en fevrier 1694." In *L'extraordinaire et le quotidien: Variations anthropologiques,* edited by Claude Allibert and Narivelo Rajaonarimanana, 479–94. Paris: Karthala.

Mondain, G. 1910. *L'histoire des tribus de l'Imoro au XVIIe siècle d'après un manuscrit arabico-malgache.* Paris: Ernest Leroux.

Mouzard, Thomas. 2011. "Territoire, trajectoire, réseau: Créativité rituelle populaire, identification et État postcolonial (Une triple étude de cas malgache)." PhD diss., École des Hautes Études en Sciences Sociales (EHESS).

Nielssen, Hilde. 2012. *Ritual Imagination: A Study of Tromba Possession Among the Betsimisaraka in Eastern Madagascar.* Leiden: Brill.

Nutting, P. Bradley. 1978. "The Madagascar Connection: Parliament and Piracy, 1690–1701." *American Journal of Legal History* 22 (3): 202–15.

Ottino, Paul. 1974. *Madagascar, les Comores et le Sud-Ouest de l'océan Indien,* Antananarivo: Université de Madagascar.

———. 1976. "Le Moyen-Age de l'océan Indien et les composantes du peuplement de Madagascar." *Asie du Sud-Est et du Monde Insulindien* 7 (2–3): 3–8.

———. 1981. "La mythologie malgache des hautes terres et le cycle politique des Andriambahoaka." In *Dictionnaire des mythologies et des religions des sociétés traditionnelles et du monde antique,* vol. 2, edited by Yves Bonnefoy, 30–45. Paris: Flammarion.

———. 1983a. "Les Andriambahoaka malgaches et l'héritage indonésien: Mythe et histoire." In *Les souverains de Madagascar: L'histoire royale et ses résurgences contemporaines,* edited by Françoise Raison-Jourde, 71–96. Paris: Karthala.

———. 1983b. "L'ancienne succession dynastique malgache (l'exemple merina)." In *Les souverains de Madagascar: L'histoire royale et ses résurgences contemporaines,* edited by Françoise Raison-Jourde, 223–63. Paris: Karthala.

———. 1986. *L'étrangère intime: Essai d'anthropologie de la civilisation de l'ancien Madagascar.* 2 vols. Paris: Editions des archives contemporaines.

Pearson, Mike Parker. 1996. "Reassessing 'Robert Drury's Journal' as a Historical Source for Southern Madagascar." *History in Africa* 23: 233–56.

———. 1997. "Close Encounters of the Worst Kind: Malagasy Resistance and Colonial Disasters in Southern Madagascar." *World Archaeology* 28 (3): 393–417.

Pennell, C. R. 1998. "Who Needs Pirate Heroes?" *The Northern Mariner/ Le marin du nord* 8 (2): 61–79.

Pérotin-Dumon, Anne, 1991. "The Pirate and the Emperor: Power and the Law on the Seas, 1450–1850." In *The Political Economy of Merchant Empires*, edited by James D. Tracy, 197–200. Cambridge: Cambridge University Press.

Petit, Michel. 1966. *La plaine littorale de Maroantsetra, étude géographique.* Antananarivo: Bureau pour le développement de la production agricole.

———. 1967. "Les Zafirabay de la baie d'Antongil (formation et histoire d'un clan, conséquences sur la vie rurale actuelle)." *Annales de l'Université de Madagascar* 7: 21–44.

Petit, Michel, and Guy Jacob. 1965. "Un essai de colonisation dans la baie d'Antongil." *Annales de l'Université de Madagascar* 4: 33–56.

Rahatoka, Salomon. 1984. "Pensée religieuse et rituels betsimisaraka." In *Ny razana tsy mba maty Cultures traditionnelles malgaches*, edited by J.-P. Domenichini et al., 31–92. Antananarivo: Ed. Librairie de Madagascar.

Rajaonarimanana, Narivelo. 1990. *Savoirs arabico-malgaches: La tradition manuscrite des devins Antemoro Anakara (Madagascar).* Paris: Institut National des Langues et Civilisations Orientales.

Randrianja, Solofo, and Stephen Ellis. 2009. *Madagascar: A Short History.* Chicago: University of Chicago Press.

Rantoandro, G. A. 2001. "Hommes et réseaux Malata de la côte orientale de Madagascar à l'époque de Jean René (1773–1826)." *Annuaire des pays de l'océan Indien* 17: 103–21.

Ratsivalaka, Gilbert. 1977. "Elements de biography de Nicolas Mayeur." *Omaly sy Anio* 5–6: 79–88.

———. 1995. *Madagascar dans le sud-ouest de l'océan Indien, c. 1500–1824.* Lille: Atelier national de reproduction des thèses.

———. 1999. *Les malgaches et l'abolition de la traite européene des esclaves, 1810–1817: Histoire de la formation du royaume de Madagascar.* Antananarivo: Imprimerie CNAPMAD

Ravelonantoandro, Andrianarison. 2010. "Les pouvoirs divinatoires des Antedoany de Fénérive-Est." ENS de philosophie de Toliara.

Ravololomanga, Bodo. 1993. *Etre femme et mère à Madagascar (Tanala d'Ifanadiana)*. Paris: Harmattan.

Rediker, Marcus. 1987. *Between the Devil and the Deep Blue Sea: Merchant Seamen, Pirates, and the Anglo-American Maritime World, 1700–1750*. Cambridge: Cambridge University Press.

———. 2004. *Villains of All Nations: Atlantic Pirates in the Golden Age.* London: Verso.

Renel, Charles. 1910. *Contes de Madagascar.* Paris: E. Leroux.

———. 1915. "Amulettes malgaches, ody et sampy." *Bulletin de l'Académie Malgache* (n.s.) 2: 29–281.

———. 1923. *Ancêtres et Dieux.* Antananarivo: G. Pitot de la Beaujardière.

Risso, Patricia. 2001. "Cross-Cultural Perceptions of Piracy: Maritime Violence in the Western Indian Ocean and Persian Gulf During a Long Eighteenth Century." *Journal of World History* 12 (2): 297–300.

Rochon, Abbé Alexis-Marie. 1792. *Voyage to Madagascar and the East Indies.* London: G. G. Robinson.

Rogoziński, Jan. 2000. *Honor Among Thieves: Captain Kidd, Henry Every, and the Pirate Democracy in the Indian Ocean.* Mechanicsburg, PA: Stackpole.

Rombaka, Jacques Philippe. 1970. *Fomban-dRazana Antemoro.* Fianarantsoa: Ambozontany.

Sahlins, Marshall. 1981. "The Stranger-King: Or Dumézil Among the Fijians." *The Journal of Pacific History* 16 (3): 107–32.

———. 2008. "The Stranger-King: Or, Elementary Forms of the Politics of Life." *Indonesia and the Malay World* 36 (105): 177–99.

———. 2013. "On the Culture of Material Value and the Cosmography of Riches." *HAU: Journal of Ethnographic Theory* 3 (2): 161–95.

Schnepel, Burkhard. 2014. "Piracy in the Indian Ocean (ca. 1680–1750)." Working paper no. 60, Max Planck Institute for Social Anthropology Working Papers, Max Planck Institute, Halle.

Sibree, James. 1880. *The Great African Island.* London: Trübner & Sons.

Snelders, Stephen. 2005. *The Devil's Anarchy.* New York: Autonomedia.

Sylla, Yvette. 1985. "Les Malata: Cohésion et disparité d'un 'groupe.'" *Omaly sy Anio* 21–2: 19–32.

Toto, Chaplain T. 2005. "Quelques aspects des expériences européennes sur la baie d'Antongil—Madagascar du XVIe au XIXe siècle." *Revue de l'Association Historique Internationale de l'Océan Indien* 1: 7–16.

Valette, Jean. 1967. "Note sur une coutume betsimisaraka du XVIIIe siècle: Les vadinebazaha." *Cahiers du Centre d'étude des coutumes* 3: 49–55.

Vérin, Pierre. 1986. *The History of Civilisation in North Madagascar.* Rotterdam: A. A. Balkema.

Vérin, Pierre, and Narivelo Rajaonarimanana. 1991. "Divination in Madagascar: The Antemoro Case and the Diffusion of Divination." In *African Divination Systems*, edited by Philip M. Peek. Bloomington: Indiana University Press.

Vig, Lars. 1969. *Charmes: Spécimens de magie malgache.* Oslo: Universitetsforlaget.

Vink, Markus. 2003. "'The World's Oldest Trade': Dutch Slavery and Slave Trade in the Indian Ocean in the Seventeenth Century." *Journal of World History* 14 (2): 131–77.

Wanner, Michal. 2008. "The Madagascar Pirates in the Strategic Plans of Swedish and Russian Diplomacy, 1680–1730." In *Prague Papers on the History of International Relations*, 73–94. Prague: Institute of World History.

Williams, Eric. 1944. *Capitalism and Slavery.* Chapel Hill: University of North Carolina Press.

Wilson, Peter Lamborn. 1995. *Pirate Utopias: Moorish Corsairs and European Renegadoes.* New York: Autonomedia.

Wilson-Fall, Wendy. 2011. "Women Merchants and Slave Depots: St. Louis, Senegal and St. Mary's, Madagascar." In *Slaving Paths: Rebuilding and Rethinking the Atlantic Worlds*, edited by Ana Lucia Araujo, 272–302. Amherst, MA: Cambria Press.

Wright, Henry T. 2006. "Early State Dynamics as Political Experiment." *Journal of Anthropological Research* 62 (3): 305–19.

Wright, Henry T., and Fulgence Fanony. 1992. "L'évolution des systèmes d'occupation des sols dan la vallée de la rivière Mananara au nord-est de Madagascar." *Taloha* 11: 47–60.